BUDDHISM IN CHINA

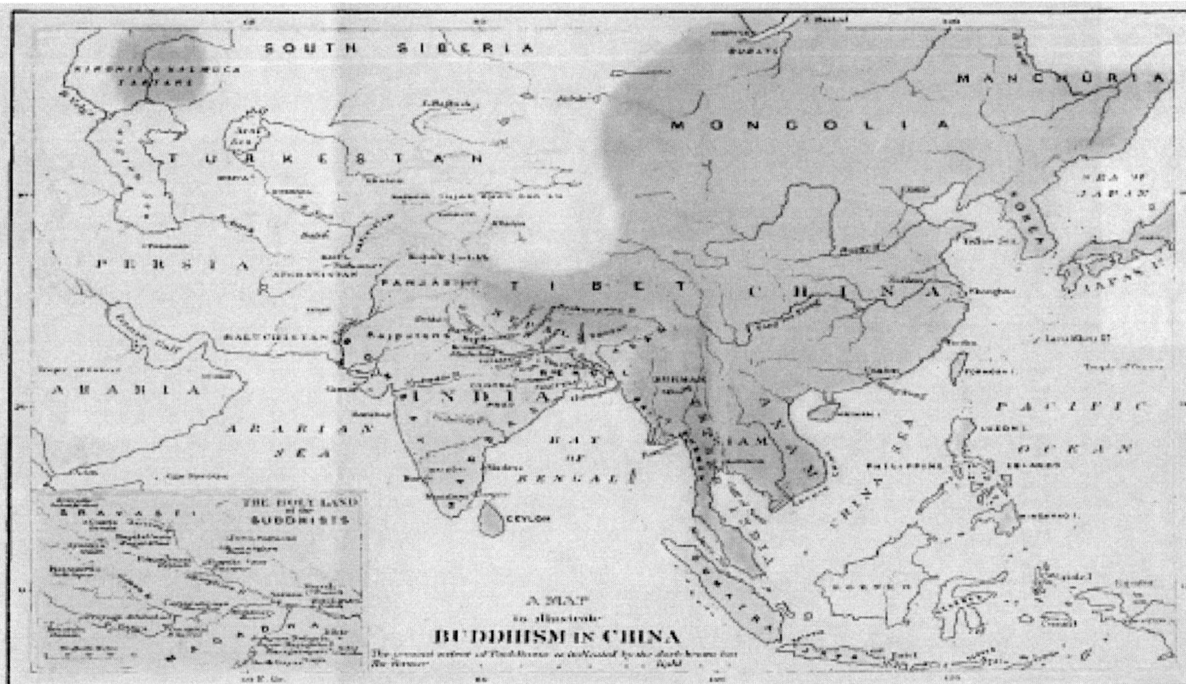

London. Published by the Society for Promoting Christian Knowledge.

NON-CHRISTIAN RELIGIONS SYSTEMS

BUDDHISM IN CHINA

BY

THE REV. S. BEAL

RECTOR OF WORK-ON-TYNE, NORTHUMBERLAND.

PUBLISHED UNDER THE DIRECTION OF THE COMMITTEE OF GENERAL LITERATURE AND EDUCATION APPOINTED BY THE SOCIETY FOR PROMOTING CHRISTIAN KNOWLEDGE.

GYAN

Published by

GYAN

Gyan Publishing House
5, Ansari Road
Daryaganj, New Delhi-110002
Phone: 011-47034999, 9811692060
E-mail: books@gyanbooks.com

Distribution Network
gyanbooks.com
India, USA, Canada, UK, Australia, France

ISBN : 978-81-212-3165-7 (PB)
First Published, 1884

2nd Impression 2020

Printed at: Gyan Press, Delhi.

Buddhism in China
Author: Beal, Samuel

Non-Christian Religious Systems.

BUDDHISM IN CHINA.

BY

THE REV. S. BEAL,

RECTOR OF WARK-ON-TYNE, NORTHUMBERLAND.

PUBLISHED UNDER THE DIRECTION OF
THE COMMITTEE OF GENERAL LITERATURE AND EDUCATION
APPOINTED BY THE
SOCIETY FOR PROMOTING CHRISTIAN KNOWLEDGE.

LONDON:
SOCIETY FOR PROMOTING CHRISTIAN KNOWLEDGE,
NORTHUMBERLAND AVENUE, CHARING CROSS, W.C.
43, QUEEN VICTORIA STREET, E.C.
26, ST. GEORGE'S PLACE, HYDE PARK CORNER, S.W.
BRIGHTON: 135, NORTH STREET.
NEW YORK: E. & J. B. YOUNG & CO.
1884.

CONTENTS.

CHAPTER VI.

CHAPTER VII.

CHAPTER VIII.

CHAPTER IX.

CHAPTER X.

CHAPTER XI.

CHAPTER XII.

CHAPTER XIII.

CHAPTER XIV.

CHAPTER XV.

CHAPTER XVI.

CHAPTER XVII.

CHAPTER XVIII.

CHAPTER XIX.

CHAPTER XX.

CHAPTER XXI.

CHAPTER XXII.

CHAPTER XXIII.

CHAPTER XXIV.

CHAPTER XXV.

BUDDHISM IN CHINA.

CHAPTER I.

INTRODUCTORY.

§ 1. Of the three religions, or religious persuasions, professed in China, two have already been described in a volume of the present series.[1]

The third, Buddhism, is to be considered in the following pages. To understand the position which this religion holds in China, it must be borne in mind that its influence depends not so much on its recognised authority as on the tone which it has given to the religious thought of the people. Although it was formerly patronised by the emperors and the court, it is now proscribed. Yet, in the presence of this, its influence is everywhere felt, and it undoubtedly affects the whole religious condition of the empire.[2] Hence it is not erroneous to include in the number of professed Buddhists throughout the Eastern world the great proportion of the Chinese people, who, if not professed disciples, are at least implicit

[1] "Confucianism and Taouism," by R. K. Douglas.

[2] Edkin's "Religion in China," p. 58.

believers in the leading facts of this religion, and conform themselves to its teaching in daily life.

The result of the co-existence of the three religious systems for so many years has been, indeed, to obliterate the distinctive features of each separately. The worship of Pu-sah, in the houses of the rich and poor, is hardly recognised as Buddhist in its origin; and, indeed, the very term Pu-sah, which is the Chinese form of Bodhisattva, is explained in the ordinary language as of native origin, and signifying "universal benevolence," whilst the objects of Buddhist worship, such as the "Goddess of Mercy" and the "Queen of Heaven," have been placed among the number of their genii, and, in the case of the former,[1] at least, attributed to their own country. Hence, again, the images of their Bodhisattvas, or Pu-sahs, are to be found in the houses of the people and the officers of government, who would strongly object to be called Buddhists. At the capture of Canton, in 1858, a large golden image of Kwan-yin was found in a shrine in an inner room of the Yamên of Yeh Ming-shin, the governor of the province. The same official had, about two years before the loss of the city, written to the emperor to state that on one occasion, at a critical juncture, whilst engaged in exterminating a band of roving plunderers, "a large figure in white had been seen beckoning to the army from the sky." This was Kwan-yin; the soldiers were inspired with courage, and won an easy victory over the enemy.[2] We are not surprised to

[1] Eitel, "Handbook," *sub* "Avalokiteśvara."

[2] Edkin's "Religion in China," p. 127.

find that one of the largest temples in the city of Canton dedicated to Kwan-yin, "who came flying from heaven" to defend the town from the first attack of the English, was mainly restored by the exertions of the chief officers of the neighbourhood, and regarded as the source of security to the inhabitants at the time of the second siege of the city. In this way we may understand how the Buddhist religion has affected the entire population of the country, and, although not supported or countenanced by the Government, is yet secretly respected even by the highest functionaries of the state.

So much, then, as to the general influence of this religion in explanation of the statement often made, that the Chinese are Buddhists. Independently of this general conformity, however, there is a large proportion of the population professedly Buddhist. What this number may be we have no means of ascertaining, but in every town and village, so far as we know, there are to be found some; and, in many cases, a Buddhist temple or temples may be seen, with numerous worshippers, so that China undoubtedly contributes to the total of Buddhists throughout the world a large proportion.

Notwithstanding our improved acquaintance with the country, however, it is discouraging to the find that our actual knowledge of the Buddhist community there is very limited. The monasteries are visited, but there is little information given about the condition of the priests, or their mode of teaching, or the character of their distinctive doctrine, so that for the purpose of this treatise we shall have to depend on the books which embody the doctrine more than the actual working of the system or the mode of enforcing the doctrine on its adherents. And in this respect we have an abundant supply of materials; in every large monastery is to be found the collection of books published and printed at the royal mandate, composing what is called the "threefold treasure," or the Tripiṭaka. In these books we find translations of Indian and other works, and native commentaries relating to the teaching of the various schools of the religion. Besides this, there is a large circulation amongst the people of tracts and treatises relating to the more popular forms of worship and belief, so that the material is, as we said, abundant for a knowledge of the system as it is taught in their books, and as this is the surest guide in all cases where practices may vary according to circumstances, we shall rely principally on it in our further inquiry on the subject.

CLASSIFICATION OF BOOKS.

§ 2. Buddhist literature is ordinarily classified under two great heads or divisions, viz., northern and southern. This partition is unknown to the Buddhists themselves; but it is a convenient one. In the first place, it was supposed to denote the division of the books under the two heads, Pāli and Sanscrit. The former represented the southern literature, the latter the northern. This, however, is not found to be the case, for the books taken to China were certainly not all of them Sanscrit, but rather composed in various dialects, and it is well known that many of the Tibetan works have been translated from Pāli. Moreover, it is stated that Pāli texts to this day are to be found in Japan, and if further search were made in the neighbourhood of Loyang (Honan fu), in China, there is good reason to believe similar texts might be found there. The division, then, of Buddhism into the so-called northern and southern schools does not depend on the sharp distinction alluded to, but rather denotes the difference between the primitive and the mixed, or developed system, as known respectively from the Pāli Scriptures in the south, and the mixed books, Sanscrit, Pāli, and other Prakrits, in the north.

§ 3. There is another division which is constantly referred to in Buddhist literature which is equally useful, but yet unknown, at least, to the southern school; this is the classification known as the Great and the Little Vehicle. We find this division referred to in the northern books of a late date; but, being unknown in southern canonical books, we conclude it came into use after those books were written, and the separation between the northern and southern school of thought completed. The Little Vehicle may be said to represent the teaching of the early Buddhists. It is called "little," or "imperfect" (hina), because it affords means of salvation to "the few" only, *i.e.*, those within the limits of the community; whereas the great, or complete, vehicle (means of conveyance,—to wit, over the sea of sorrow, or the world holds out the assurance of safety or deliverance to all. The formula in the first instance is, "all those that are to be saved, are saved"; in the second, "all that are not saved, shall be saved," viz., by the bequeathed law or doctrine preached in the world. We cannot venture to define exhaustively the further differences between these two systems. It may be accepted as generally true, that the early school knew nothing of the distinctions that arose at a later period and caused the classification we are now speaking about. But yet, it was well recognised by the Buddhists themselves, when the developed system was shaped by the writers of *S̀âstras* and others, who lived principally in North India towards the close of the first century B.C., and later; and, therefore, we meet with the terms "Little" and "Great Vehicle" constantly in the travels of the Chinese Pilgrims,[1] and in the controversial works of the scholastic period of Buddhist history.

§ 4. The great and fundamental division of the system, however, occurred about one hundred years after the death of its founder. In order to make this point as clear as possible, it will be necessary to allude briefly to the early history of the system, leaving a more particular account of it, as we find it in the later books, for subsequent notice.

The date of Buddha's death has been variously computed from data which may, for the present, be confined to the southern records, as occurring between 543 B.C. and 412 B.C.[2] One hundred years after his Nirvāna, a schism arose in the Sañgha,[3] resulting from neglect of discipline among some Bhikshus (mem-

[1] Hiouen Thsang, and Fa Hian.

[2] Rhys Davids' "Numismata Orientalia," p. 55.

[3] The Buddhist community.

bers of the Buddhist community) living at Vaisâli, a town not far to the north of Patna. The lay members of the community in this place had been induced by the Bhikshus to give them money,[1] which was divided at stated periods among the disciples. This liberty of possessing money was in contradiction to the rules of the order. A leading member of the brotherhood, named Yasa, protested against this violation of discipline, and in consequence was expelled from the community by an act (*kamma*) of the brotherhood of Vaisâli. In consequence of this, he brought before the notice of the leading brethren (*Sthaviras*) resident in other places ten faults or sins which had crept in among the Vaisâli priests, and, having settled the question as to their non-legality, a council was summoned, under the presidency of Revata, to stamp the offences with its disapprobation, and root out the offenders from the society. This was the cause of the great schism from which the minor divisions that afterwards occurred must be traced. The practices of the Vaisâli brethren were condemned, and the purity of the rules of the order vindicated. Whether the sacred books were written at this time, or not, we cannot know positively, but in any case it is very probable that they were recited in the convocation with a view to establish the primitive discipline; they were then handed down in that form in the school that represented the orthodox party of the council. This party was called "the followers of the Sthaviras" or "elders." The other section of the community,

[1] "Abstract of Four Lectures," p. 83.

headed by the Vaisâli party of priests, formed their own body, and were called the Mahâsañghikas, or "great congregation." In these two bodies was kept the knowledge of the early tenets of Buddhism, according to their determination at this time. Undoubtedly, the more reliable form is that preserved in the Sthavira school; the tenets of the "great congregation" were adapted to the looser discipline and less accurate knowledge of the Vaisâli priests. It may be stated broadly, that the Pāli Scriptures embody the doctrine of the Sthaviras or elders, whilst the northern books are, more or less, derived from the teaching of the popular party, known as the Mahâsañghikas. We know little about the history of Buddhism previous to the meeting of this council. The common account is that an earlier assembly had been held near Râjagriha, shortly after Buddha's death, in which the canon of the sacred writings had been fixed, and the place where, and occasion on which, each discourse had been delivered, or each rule enacted, precisely laid down. This first council, called that of the 500, is not, as now stated, historical. We may, however, suppose that there was some agreement between the leading members of the order, as to their rules of discipline and doctrines, on the decease of the master. But, beyond the light afforded us at the opening of the period belonging to the council at Vaisâli, we know nothing of the events of the hundred years that had elapsed between these two points. We gather, from the account given us of the errors of the priests, that each town had its own customs, and that the community was bound together, at this time at least, by no well-understood discipline. Leading members of the order had fixed their abodes at spots of their own selection, and to them resorted, on emergency, teachers or learners to have their doubts settled, whilst they themselves were attended by a body of disciples who followed them where they went and received from them daily instruction. Thus we find Revata in the company of a select body of followers when Yasa came to consult him on the Vaisâli heresy, and the older teachers who came with Revata to the council must have brought with them their attendants or disciples, who thus swelled the number of the assembly to its traditional complement of 700. This being the first historical event in the Buddhist history, it was thought better to state so much, at least, respecting it.

CHAPTER II.

WHENCE OUR KNOWLEDGE OF THE NORTHERN BOOKS HAS BEEN DERIVED.

§ 1. We must briefly allude to the character of the materials from which our knowledge of Northern Buddhism is derived. For this end we will mention the three great groups of books which have been discovered and partly examined during the last half century. These are (1) the Sanscrit works found in Nepal; (2) the Tibetan books, generally styled the *Ká-gyur* or *Kán-gyur;* and (3) the Chinese *San-ts'ong*, or Tripiṭaka.

With regard to the Sanscrit works of Nepal, which are generally supposed to have been the origin of the "northern" translations, the discovery of these is due to Mr. Brian Houghton Hodgson. This gentleman, in 1820, was appointed assistant to the English Resident at Khatmandu, the chief town of Nepal. He afterwards became himself the Resident, and his career in that office extended from A.D. 1833 to the close of 1843. Altogether, his sojourn in Nepal lasted through a period of twenty-one years. During this period he devoted himself to earnest inquiry as to the physical character of the country in which he lived, and the condition and religion of the people. Before his time our knowledge of Buddhism was of the thinnest character possible. Even Dr. Marshman, who lived in India and was in every way so ripe a scholar, in his Chinese grammar, published at Serampore (1824), could give no better account of Buddha than that his worship was probably connected with the Egyptian Apis. And on every hand we find theories of the most grotesque kind started to explain the origin and nature of this mysterious religion. Mr. Hodgson, however, took up the matter at first hand, and, with his native Bauddha teacher by his side, drew up a scheme of the religion as accepted in Nepal, which, when published in the "Transactions" of the Royal Asiatic Society, completely upset the theories which had hitherto been prevalent on the subject, and shed a new light on the matter. Quoting from the pages of Dr. Rájendralála Mitra,[1] "Mr. Hodgson's researches into religion are limited to that form of it which prevails in Nepal,—the Buddhism of Sâkya Siñha, as it developed itself in that Alpine region on its expulsion from Hindustan,—but he has done more on that subject than any other European writer. Before his time, all that was known of Buddhism was crude, vague, and shadowy, derived from secondary and by no means reliable sources. It is he who established the subject on a sound philosophic basis. Altogether, he wrote eighteen papers on the subject, and they are replete with the most varied and instructive information. Much has been done since; but no one can even now write on Buddhism with any accuracy who has not thoroughly

[1] "The Sanscrit Buddhist Literature of Nepal," p. xii., Calcutta, 1882.

studied Mr. Hodgson's essays." Without alluding further to the work done by Mr. Hodgson, we will state the result of his investigations as briefly as possible. He found, then, that in the valley of Nepal there was a collection of Sanscrit Buddhist books, which, before his time, were perfectly unknown. Quoting again from Dr. Ráj. Mitra :[1] "His discovery has entirely revolutionised the history of Buddhism as it was known to Europeans in the early part of this century. The total number of books discovered is not stated, but it is believed that the works when carefully arranged and indexed will amount to about two hundred. Copies of these works to the total number of 381 bundles have been distributed so as to render them accessible to European scholars. Of these 85 bundles, comprising 144 separate works, were presented to the Asiatic Society of Bengal; 85 to the Royal Asiatic Society of London; 30 to the India Office Library; 7 to the Bodleian Library, Oxford; and 174 to the Société Asiatique in Paris, or to M. Burnouf personally. This last collection is now deposited in the Bibliothèque Nationale of France." The character of these works was first noticed by Mr. Hodgson, in his "Essays."[2] He was thus not only the discoverer of these ancient and authentic records, but also the first intelligent exponent of their nature and value, both in their ritualistic and philosophical aspects.

[1] *Op. cit.*, xxiv.

[2] Since published separately,—"Essays on the Languages, Literature, and Religion of Nepál and Tibet," by B. H. Hodgson, Esq., Trübner, 1874.

The outcome of this discovery was shown first of all in the enthusiasm excited in France on the subject. Mr. Hodgson entered at once into the arena as a controversialist, especially with Abel Rémusat, who appeared to question some of the deductions drawn from Mr. Hodgson's examination of the Nepalese books. But this soon passed by, and the more solid result of the discovery was shown in the publication of two works by M. Eugène Burnouf: first, the "Introduction to the History of Indian Buddhism," in 1844; and, secondly, "The Lotus of the Good Law," translated from the Sanscrit, in 1852. These two works remain the foundation of our knowledge of Northern Buddhism. They were the first books published in Europe claiming to exhibit the system in its real character, and they are still the best authority upon the question. M. Burnouf gracefully dedicated the second of these works to Mr. Hodgson, as the founder of the true study of Buddhism. Speaking generally, the points established by the discovery of these works are these:—(1) That Buddhist books were written at an early date in Sanscrit. (2) That the works so written were not translations from the Pāli, or the southern language of Magadha, but original compositions, for they are not known in the south; and (3) that they contain a system of expanded doctrine, alien in many points from the spirit of early Buddhism, and principally of a philosophic or mystic character.

It would be impossible in a work like this to enter on an examination of the doctrine of this school of Buddhism. For those who wish to do so, however, Mr. Hodgson's own "Essays"[1] are still the best guide, supplemented by the researches of M. Burnouf.

§ 2. Secondly, with respect to the Tibetan books,—these also were discovered, in the first instance, by Mr. Hodgson. They are not, strictly speaking, books, but xylographs, being inscribed on wooden boards or splints. These works, or at least the Kágyur, or Kángyur, include no less than 100 volumes, arranged under the three heads of Dulva, Do, and Sherchin, whence their common name De-not-sum, or, in Sanscrit, Tripiṭaka—"the three repositories, or baskets." The name Kágyur means "translations of commandments," and the works are avowed to be translations of texts existing between the seventh and thirteenth centuries, in the language of Magadha. But, although Mr. Hodgson procured on his own account, and, as it appears, independently, copies of these works, our knowledge of their contents is due to the singular zeal and devotion of a simple Hungarian student, Mr. Alexander Csoma Körösi (so he signed himself in English, the word Körösi being an adjectival form, signifying "of Körös"). He was the son of a military family of Egerpatak, in the Transylvanian circle of Hungary.[2] After having been educated for the Church, and having studied at Göttingen under Gottfried Eickhorn, he made up his mind to devote his life to the study of Eastern languages. So he set forth from Bucharest on the 1st of January, 1820,

[1] *Op. cit.*

[2] For this and what follows I am indebted to Mr. Ralston's "Tibetan Tales," Introduction.

without friends or money, travelling on foot or by water on a raft till he reached Bagdad. Thence he pushed on to Teheran, where he spent four months. In March, 1821, he again started with a caravan, travelling as an American, and, after a stay of six months in Khorasàn, arrived in the middle of November at Bokhara. There he intended to pass the winter, but, alarmed by the reported approach of a numerous Russian army, he travelled with a caravan to Kabul, where he arrived early in 1822. At the end of a fortnight he again set out, and, coming to Lahore, obtained permission to visit Kashmir; thence he travelled on to Ladák, where he finally settled with Mr. Moorcroft, who lent him the "Alphabetum Tibetanum," published at Rome in 1762, and compiled by Father Antonio Agostino Georgi. The perusal of this book determined him to study Tibetan. Accordingly, in 1824, we find him sojourning at Zanskár (in the province of Ladák), working with a Làma. After this he arrived at Sabathú, in British India. Thence he travelled again into Western Tibet, where he continued till 1831: in the autumn of this year he was at Simla, "dressed in a coarse blue cloth loose gown, extending to his heels, and a small cloth cap of the same material. He wore a grizzly beard, shunned the society of Europeans, and passed his whole time in study."[1] In May, 1832, he went to Calcutta, where he met with great kindness from many scholars, especially Professor H. H. Wilson and Mr. James Prinsep. Here he resided during many years, and published his two principal works, the "Essay

[1] *Op. cit.*, p. xiv.

towards a Dictionary, Tibetan and English,"[1] and "A Grammar of the Tibetan Language."

Finally, in 1842, he left Calcutta with a view to find his way to Lhasa; but, arriving at Darjíling, in Nepal, he was attacked by fever, and on the 6th of April in that year he died, a victim, as Professor Max Müller has said, "to his heroic devotion to the study of ancient languages and religions."[2]

We have thought it only due to the memory of this singularly devoted student to say thus much as to his career. With respect to his work on the Tibetan Buddhist books, we may find all information necessary for the purpose of this outline in the first part of the XXth volume of "Asiatic Researches."[3] Speaking of the great compilation of Tibetan sacred books, Mr. A. Csoma says:—"These books contain the doctrine of Shâkya Buddha, and were compiled at three different times and in three different places in India. First, immediately after the death of Shâkya; afterwards, in the time of Ashoka, 110 years after the decease of Shâkya; and, lastly, in the time of Kanishka, a king in the north of India, upwards of 400 years from Shâkya. These works were imported nto Tibet, and translated there between the seventh and thirteenth century of our era, but mostly in the ninth." Without attempting to explain the number or character of these works, we may state, as a general conclusion, that they were not translated solely from Sanscrit, but from various Prakrits, and especially Pāli. That they differ from the works of Nepal, inasmuch as they assume the form of the three-fold

[1] Ralston, xvi. [2] Ralston, xviii. [3] Calcutta, 1836.

collection (Tripiṭaka) known in the south, and include many of the same books. One marked feature, with reference to these books, is that the whole of the Vinaya, or code of discipline, is found among them, whereas these are absent in the Nepalese collection,—the latter, in fact, being almost exclusively made up of scholastic or philosophical treatises of a comparatively late date. Since the time of Mr. Csoma, many labourers have worked in the same field of Tibetan literature, but we need not name these; sufficient to know that the Buddhist books of Tibet are in the main derived from the same sources as those found in China, about which we now come to speak.

§ 3. It had been long known, principally through the papers written by Dr. Edkins in the "Shanghai Almanack," that the Buddhist Tripiṭaka was to be found in the great monasteries of China. But no attempt was made to procure these books in England, until the interest aroused by the discoveries already made in Nepal and Tibet excited some curiosity on the point. This was greatly increased by the publication of the translation from the Chinese of the travels of one of the Chinese Buddhist pilgrims who visited India in the beginning of the fifth century of our era, by M. Abel Rémusat, in 1836.[1] Here, for the first time, it was found that there were books in China relating to India in the early period of the Christian era, which might throw a flood of light on its history. This interest was greatly increased when M. Stas. Julien published, in 1858, his concluding volume relating to the life and travels of

[1] "Fo Koue Ki," Paris, 1836.

another pilgrim from China, called Hiouen Thsang. It may safely be said that these books created a new opinion in Europe with reference to Chinese literature and to some extent with reference to the Chinese people. It was hard to believe that such enthusiasm and devotion could have been found in natives of that country as are so eminently conspicuous in the character of these pilgrims. Besides this, the history and chronology of India were illustrated in a remarkable degree by their memoirs, insomuch that it has been said by one able to judge, that "the voyages of two Chinese travellers, undertaken in the fifth and seventh centuries of our era, have done more to elucidate the history and geography of India than all that has hitherto been found in the Sanscrit and Pāli books of that and the neighbouring countries."[1] This interest in Chinese Buddhism having been aroused, several students entered the field, and have contributed to our further knowledge of the subject. But it was felt that until we had the very books before us which form the sacred writings of Buddhism in China we should not be able to arrive at any final judgment on the question. The present writer was fortunate enough to be the means of procuring these works as they now stand on the shelves of the India Office Library. He had been led to a consideration of the question of Buddhism in China during a temporary residence in that country and in Japan in the years 1854–9. The number of monasteries in such a little Japanese town as Hakodate (in Yezo), and the remarkable character of the discipline and services followed in

[1] Bishop Bigandet, "Life of Gaudama," 1868.

these establishments, first drew his serious attention to the subject. It was plain to him that no real work could be done among the people by missions until the system of their belief was understood, and the system could not be fairly understood until we had their books.

Accordingly, application was made through the India Office[1] to our minister at Pekin, to urge the Chinese Government to allow either the purchase of the Tripiṭaka, as it is known in that country, or to procure the books as a free gift. But these attempts were unsuccessful, owing to the strained relationship existing at that time between the Chinese Government and the Western powers. On the occasion of the Japanese ambassador, Iwakura-Tomomi, visiting this country, the same request was made to him. The Japanese, it was known, had adopted Buddhism from China, through Korea, and the books they possessed had all come to them from this direction. The ambassador at once acceded to the request, and on his return to Tôkio ordered the whole collection of the books, known as "The Sacred Teaching of the Three Treasures," printed during the great Ming dynasty, in China, to be forwarded to this country. With respect to these books, which form the basis of the Buddhist religion both in China and Japan, I will quote from the opening pages of the Catalogue which was prepared for the India Office. "This collection was published by order of the Emperor (of China) Wan-lieh towards the end of the sixteenth century.

[1] I wish here to bear my grateful testimony to the invariable kindness and ready help of Dr. Rost, the distinguished librarian of the India Office.

It was reproduced, in Japan, in the sixth year of the Nengo (year-period) Im-po, *i.e.*, A.D. 1679, and afterwards issued with an imperial preface in the period Ten-wa, A.D. 1681–3. As first received at the India Office, the collection was contained in seven large boxes, carefully packed in lead, with padding of dry rushes and grass. The entire series of books was arranged in 103 cases or covers; in each case there were, on an average, twenty volumes, so that the entire number of volumes is more than 2,000. Placed one above the other, the books in the collection would reach to a height of about 110 feet."[1] This body of literature represents the entire series of sacred books taken during successive years from India to China and there translated, as well as the works of native Chinese priests, with commentaries, catalogues, and indexes. Here, then, is the groundwork of our knowledge of the Buddhist religion in China and Japan. It is plain that it will require many years before we can arrive at a correct estimate of the character of these books, or their value as authentic translations. But, so far as is yet known, they contain valuable materials for a knowledge of Buddhism in all its periods of expansion or development, from the simple creed taught in the first instance by its founder down to the subtle and fine-drawn doctrine of the latest period of scholastic development.

As a brief summary, sufficient for present purposes, we will again quote from the Catalogue already referred to. First of all, it may be well to state that the term

[1] Beal's catalogue of the Buddhist Tripiṭaka as known in China and Japan.

Tripiṭaka, or, in Chinese, San-ts'ong, means the three treasures or baskets. The last term may possibly allude to the mode of preserving the palm-leaves on which the sacred texts were written, viz., in baskets, or cases of basket-work. The three divisions of the texts, corresponding to the three baskets, are known as the Vinaya, or code of discipline; the Sûtras, or discourses delivered by Buddha; and the Abhidharma, or metaphysics. These terms so explained are elastic. The Vinaya sometimes contains sermons, and the Sûtras are often discourses on points of discipline, whilst the one and the other frequently assume a metaphysical character; so that the definition can only be regarded as a general one. In the Chinese collection each of these sections is fully represented. So far as we can ascertain, the Vinaya division (called by the name of Agama, as well as Vinaya) includes the books known in the southern school, and many more. There is, in fact, a Vinaya section belonging to the Great Vehicle (Mahāyana, or expanded form of Buddhist doctrine) as well as the Little Vehicle. These are given in the Catalogue, p. 3, and are included in five covers or *han*. The Vinaya of the lesser development, on the other hand, is included in forty-eight covers or *han*. It is amongst these that we may expect to find many of the books known to us by translations from the Pāli. With respect to the Sûtra and Abhidharma divisions, there are some already ascertained to be translations from primitive works known in the southern school; the majority are of a late date, that is, later than the time when the southern canon was finally adjusted, and therefore not found therein.

CHAPTER III.

AGREEMENT BETWEEN EARLY NORTHERN AND SOUTHERN BOOKS.

§ 1. THE inquiry as to the identity of the southern and northern books, although not ripe for final settlement, is still of such interest and importance that we may perhaps dwell on it a little longer. One thing is certain, that the southern canon surpasses any other collection of Buddhist books in point of arrangement and perspicuity. It is, in fact, on the face of it, a primitive arrangement. The northern collection, on the other hand (especially in China and Japan), is a miscellaneous and hap-hazard assortment of books, classified according to the will of the scholars who had charge of the work, with very little reference either to precedent or authority. It will, therefore, take time to establish anything like identity between the books of the two schools; but yet, as the question involved is really as to identity of fundamental belief, more than divergence in detail, it is well to mark the agreements as we find them. First, then, with respect to discipline, or the constitution of the order. There is in the north and south agreement on this point. The Pratimoksha, or, in the Pāli, Pātimokkha, is a primitive work; "it is the oldest, and in many respects the most important, material of the Vinaya literature."[1] Now, this work has been translated as well from Chinese as from Pāli, and the result shows almost an identity of character and contents. By an oversight on the part of the learned translators of the Pāli text, the translation from the Chinese is not even referred to. They say, "the text, as it lies before us, stands so well against all proofs, whether we compare its different parts one with another, or with the little that is yet known of its northern counterparts, that we are justified in regarding these Pāli books as in fact the authentic mirror of the old Magadhî text, as fixed in the central schools of the most ancient Buddhist church"; and then they add, in a note, in reference to the northern school, "How little this is [*i.e.*, our knowledge of what the northern school teaches] is apparent from the fact that Burnouf, who had studied all those books that were then accessible, did not even find the words pârâjika and saṁghadisesa (two terms occurring in the Pātimokkha)"; and then they proceed: "Of the Chinese we have only the brief notices of M. Rémusat and of Mr. Beal (in H. Oldenberg's 'Introduction to the Vinaya'). The last scholar also mentions several Vinaya works, (of the contents of which, however, nothing further is known) in his Catalogue of Chinese Buddhist works now in the India Office Library." But, as a matter of fact, the Pratimoksha had been translated by the present writer from the Chinese language so far back as the year 1859, and had been printed in an especial

[1] "Sacred Books of the East," vol. xiii., p. xxxvi.

manner side by side with Mr. Gogerly's translation from the Pāli, to show the close agreement of the two versions. Mr. Spence Hardy prefaced the paper with some remarks as to the importance of the fact thus established, viz., that the Buddhism of China and of Ceylon were, so far as this goes, in complete accord. By a comparison of the two versions, we find that the number of the rules laid down slightly varies: in the Pāli they are 227, in the Chinese, 250; but the division into sections or classes of faults requiring a different degree of penance is the same throughout. These sections are eight in number, and are classed in both schools in the following order:—

Pāli.	Chinese.
1. Pârâgika (four).	Po-lo-i (four).
2. Samghâdisesâ (thirteen).	Săng-kia-po-shi-sha (thirteen).
3. Aniyatâ (two).	Wu-teng (two).
4. Nissaggiya Pakittiya (thirty).	Ni-sa-chi-po-yeh-to (thirty).
5. Pâkittiyâ (ninety-two).	Po-yé-to (ninety).
6. Patidesamyâ (four).	Po-lo-ti-ti-che-ni (four).
7. Sekhiyâ (seventy-five).	Chung-hioh (one hundred).
8. Adhikarana-samalhâ (seven).	Mih-tsang (seven).

The order of the rules in the above comparative list is the same, and the number, under each head, varies but slightly. Under the fifth section the number in the Pāli is ninety-two, in the Chinese it is ninety. On referring to the two versions, we find that the difference arises from the absence in the Chinese of rules "four" and "five." Whether the omission was accidental or the original from which the Chinese was translated defective, or whether the two rules have crept into the Pāli version or been introduced by a particular school, we cannot decide. The absolute agreement in other points makes the divergence of less importance. As to the difference in number under the seventh head, this is found by inspection to result from the introduction of a number of rules (twenty-five) relating to reverence or decorum to be observed when near a pagoda or *stûpa*. These rules occur in the Chinese version from sixty to eighty-four, and are wanting in the Pāli. This difference is easily accounted for. The reverence for *stûpas*, and the merit of building and repairing them, was a comparatively late feature introduced after the great builder Asoka had lived and died. We do not find these rules in the Pāli, therefore, because, presumably, the Pāli version was prepared from a code of rules in existence before the time of this king. But the Chinese version was made at a later date, and probably from an original drawn up in India after Asoka's time, so that the reverence for sacred spots and buildings, which was so marked a feature in the later discipline of the order, had taken shape and found a place in the code at the time of the preparation of the version of the Pratimoksha, from which the Chinese was translated. This explanation is so far probable and satisfactory as it agrees with all the conditions of the question; for, first, it is highly probable that the Pāli copy is as old as Asoka's time, if not older; whilst, on the other hand, the reverence for sacred buildings did undoubtedly result from the zeal displayed by that monarch, who, according to the popular account, erected in one day throughout Jambudwipa 84,000 of these sacred towers. Then, again, the love of the Chinese people for these pagodas, as proved by their universal presence in the country, would naturally excite in them a desire to perpetuate a reverence for them by the adoption of such rules as they found laid down in the copy of the Pratimoksha brought to their country. With reference to the other rules, there is an exact agreement between the two schools, and the identity of the code in both cases, therefore, seems to be established.

§ 2. But it is not only in point of arrangement and number, but also in respect to ritual and matter that this agreement is seen. The theory was, that there should be a general assembly of the Sañgha, or congregation, twice during each month,—viz., at the new moon and full moon,—and that then, after certain preliminary inquiries, there should be a repetition of the rules in the order laid down, according to their character; and, after each section of rules had been repeated, that any brother who had offended in either of the particulars named should confess his fault and accept the penance allotted. If there were no offenders, then they all remained silent, and the officiating brother declared the assembly to be pure. Now, this is absolutely the same discipline observed in China as in Ceylon. To show this, I will adduce a few instances. There is an introduction in each case, not literally the same but in strict agreement. In the Chinese, the assembly is convened on the sacred day, *i.e.*, the fifteenth day of the half month,—the words are: "on this fifteenth day [or fourteenth according to the number of days in the month] of the white division, or, the dark division, of the month let the assembly [chapter] listen attentively whilst the precepts [rules] are distinctly recited." The Pāli is: "To-day is the sacred day [of the full or new moon] the fifteenth day of the half month. If it be convenient to the chapter, let the chapter hold *uposatha*, let it repeat the Pātimokkha." The Chinese goes on: "I desire to repeat the Pratimoksha,—if any brothers have transgressed let them repent, if no brothers have transgressed let them stand silent,— thus it shall be known ye are guiltless!" The Pāli has: "Whosoever has incurred a fault, let him declare it! if no fault have been incurred, it is meet to keep silence! Now, venerable sirs! it is by your silence I shall know whether ye are pure!" Both versions then go on to speak of the guilt of deception or lying [*i.e.* not confessing]. The Chinese says: "Buddha has declared that prevarication effectually prevents our religious advancement. That brother, therefore, who is conscious of transgression, and desires absolution, ought at once to declare his fault, and after proper penance he shall have quiet." The Pālī says: "Venerable sirs! the uttering of a deliberate lie has been declared by the blessed one to be a condition hurtful to spiritual progress. Therefore, a fault, if there be one, should be declared by that Bhikshu [brother] who remembers it, and desires to be cleansed therefrom. For a fault, when declared, shall be light to him." And so the introduction in each case continues, in parallel sections, not absolutely and literally the same (and this would be impossible in translations from languages so different as Pāli and Chinese), but sufficiently alike to show that the originals were founded on one code of discipline, established at an early period, in the primitive Buddhist church.

§ 3. But this will be yet more clear if we compare together a few rules drawn from both versions of this interesting work. For this purpose we will select some of the first rules coming under the heading Sekhiyâ dhammâ. These rules refer to decorum on the part of the Bhikshus (disciples) in their intercourse with the world, or, as it is explained in the Pāli rules, regarding matters connected with discipline. The observance of decorum in walking, sitting, and speaking, is regarded as most important by the Buddhists; and in the books there is frequent allusion made to the effect produced on observers by the dignified walk or attitude of the Bhikshus on their daily rounds when begging their food. It is no matter of surprise, therefore, that rules such as these should be found in their code of moral discipline. The first Sekhiyâ rule, according to the Pāli, is this, "I will put my under garment all round me," that is, so as to cover the body from the navel to the knee (in the Pāli "parimaṇḍalam"). The Chinese version is simply, "I will adjust my inner robe properly," which is explained in the note to mean just what the Pāli signifies. The second rule is, in the Pāli, "I will put on my robe all around me," that is, the outer robe, or sanghâṭî, for the Buddhist monk was allowed three robes (in Pāli *ticivaram*), viz., the antaravāsika, the uttarasanghâṭî, and the sanghâṭî,—of these the last was the outer one. The Chinese version gives the second rule thus: "I will adjust properly the outward robes." The third rule from the Pāli is: "Properly clad will I go amidst the houses"; from the Chinese: "Not with disordered robes will I enter the houses of laymen." The fourth rule, again, in both versions forbids a priest "to sit down in a layman's house with disordered robes"; and although the order of the rules following under this section is not the same in both, there is such agreement as to make it evident both codes were drawn from a common source.[1]

§ 4. But the agreement between the books of China and the Pāli canonical works may be traced further than this. The rules for the ordination of novices and admission to full order are identical in both cases. The service of ordination is generally conducted on a *uposatha* (Chinese *u-po*) day, *i.e.*, one of the days when the Pratimoksha is recited, or one of the alternate seventh days between the new and full moon, and *vice versâ*. The order for this service (Upasampadâ-kammavâka) has been detailed by F. Spiegel, in his translation of the Kammavakya, or ordination book, of the Buddhists.[2] It is also found, though not as a service, but in its primitive shape, as a code of directions in the Mahâvagga, of the Vinaya Piṭaka, of the southern (Pāli) school.[3] On comparison, the service as laid down in the Chinese version of the Vinaya, according to the Dharmagupta school, is found to correspond closely with the Pāli. The order is this: first, the boundary within which the

1 The reader is referred for full information on this point to the parallel versions given in the "Journal of the R.A.S."

2 "Kammavakya, Liber de Officiis Sacerdotum Buddhicorum," Bonn, 1841.

3 "Sacred Books of the East," vol. xiii.

robes may be kept and the service of ordination conducted is determined. Then the Upadhyâya (Chinese, Hoshang), spiritual director, presents the candidate for ordination. He is questioned as to his age, permission of parents, freedom from disease, debt, or other impediment. He then shows his begging-dish and vestments, and retires. Being again summoned, request having been made for his ordination in the meantime, the questions as to age (he must be above 20 years of age), absence of disease, freedom from debt, and permission of parents, are again repeated in the presence of the assembled chapter, and, being answered satisfactorily, the several vows are taken one by one, after being clearly recited, and the promise is made by the candidate to keep them absolutely. These vows are: 1. I will not kill any living thing (pâṇîtapâtâ veramaṇî). 2. I will not steal (adinnâdânâ ver.). 3. I will not commit any unclean action (adultery or even marriage) (Abrahma chariya ver.). 4. I will not lie (musâvâdâ ver.). 5. I will not drink wine or any intoxicating drink (surâmereyya majjapamâdaṭṭhânâ). 6. I will not eat at unseasonable hours (vikālabhojana ver.). 7. I will not take part in singing, dancing, musical, or theatrical performances, not witness them or listen to them (Natchchagita vâdita vîsukadassanâ ver.). 8. I will not decorate myself with flowers, nor anoint my body with perfumes. 9. I will not occupy an elevated or broad couch. 10. I will not possess, or own, or acquire, coined or uncoined money or jewels.

These are the vows taken at full ordination, and the questions, ceremonies, and sequence of service observed and explained in Chinese ritual according to the Vinaya[1] of the Dharmagupta school, appears to be identical with that given in the Kammavakya by Spiegel, and translated from the Pāli. Moreover, the order observed in the Mahâvagga, as we have it translated by Dr. Rhys Davids,[2] corresponds closely, though not entirely, with that of the Vinaya according to the Mahâsañghika school in the Chinese version;[3] for in both works we have, first of all, a brief history of Buddha, after his enlightenment, followed by rules or sections (Khandhakas) relating to various matters of discipline, and the first of these is the ordination of Novices and Bhikshus. When the Chinese Vinaya has been fully examined and translated, the agreement between the two versions of this portion of the Buddhist Tripiṭaka will be capable of determination. It would be out of the question to enter on any detailed comparison here, we are satisfied to know that there is such an agreement as to show, beyond doubt, that the Buddhist ritual in China, so far as this part of it is concerned, is derived from the same sources, and probably the same books, as those to which the southern school is indebted for theirs.

§ 5. It seems necessary to settle this inquiry, however, as to the agreement or non-agreement of the northern and southern books, as it has been discussed hitherto from one side only: I shall, therefore, proceed to make some remarks concerning the second great division of the "three treasures," or the sacred books,

[1] Catalogue, "Vinaya," Case 48.
[2] "Sacred Books of the East," vol. xiii.
[3] Catalogue, "Vinaya," Case 43.

which is the Sûtra Pitaka. The Sûtras were, in the first instance, supposed to be discourses or sermons delivered by Buddha himself. When Ânanda, the personal attendant and a relative of Buddha, was called upon in the first convocation to recite these discourses with a view to their being accepted as canonical, he began as follows:—"On a certain time, in a certain place [naming it], I heard thus." This formula, "I heard thus," became typical of the Sûtra collection of discourses; but the corruption of later times led to the invention of numberless books professing to be sermons of Buddha, and beginning in the accepted way, which could never have been recited by him, nor by any of his early followers. Thus we have a book known as the Amitābha Sûtra, which deals with the fabulous paradise of the west (about which some remarks will be made further on), an invention probably of mediæval Buddhism, after the beginning of the Christian era. In this Sûtra there is the customary formula:—"Thus have I heard. On a certain occasion, Buddha was residing, &c.," and in the Chinese commentary it is said: "Thus have I heard," that is, Ânanda heard Buddha recite the words. Now this is clearly fictitious; but in the earlier or primitive books the formula in question may really have stamped the discourse with authority. For these early Sûtras or sermons we must look to the Pāli version; and if we find similar sermons in the northern collection, we may assume that on further search the correspondence will be found more complete. Now, there are various Sûtras already translated from the Pāli which are found also in a Chinese form, somewhat changed perhaps, but agreeing to an extent that shows they were translated from a text derived from, or existing collaterally with, the southern version of the sacred books as now known in Ceylon. I will name some of these primitive Sûtras as they are found in Chinese, corresponding with others of the same name in Pāli. First of all, let us take a sermon known as the "Brahmajâla Sutta," in Pāli. The text of this discourse has been published by M. P. Grimblot,[1] and translated by the Rev. D. Gogerly, Wesleyan missionary in Ceylon. He says, in his preface, "The first reason why I have made the selection of the first sermon in the series of discourses attributed to Gotama Buddha is, that a comparison may be instituted between the sacred books of the Buddhists, as they exist in Ceylon and as they exist in Nepal." This comparison has never yet been made, because, so far as is at present known, this primitive Sûtra has not been found among the Nepalese books: it is not, at least, in the list given by Dr. Ráj. Mitra in his examination of the Nepalese Buddhist literature. But in the Chinese Tripiṭaka, two works bearing the name Brahmajâla have been discovered.[2] The first is a book of a late date and purely fictitious: it relates to the conduct of the Bodhisattva, and has nothing in common (except the name) with the southern Sûtra as translated by Gogerly. But there is another work in the Tripiṭaka in China, called "Fan-kong

[1] "Sept Suttas Pâlis," Paris, 1876.

[2] Beal's "Report," September, 1874, No. 2. Transactions of the first Oriental Congress held in London.

luh shih 'rh kien," that is, "The sixty-two heretical views contained in the Brahmajâla Sûtra,"[1] which on examination turns out to be a version of the same text as we have before us in M. Grimblot's book. We can only compare a few passages. The Chinese begins thus:—"Thus have I heard, Buddha was passing through the Kuru country with his great disciples, 1,250 in all; at this time the Paribbâjaka (taou jin) Suppiya (Su-pi), accompanied by his attendant, Brahmadatta Manava, followed Buddha and the Bhikshus along the road, at which time Suppiya and his followers reviled Buddha, and his doctrine, and the priesthood; whilst his disciple, Brahmadatta Manava, praised Buddha, and his law and the priesthood. And thus the master and his disciple continued disputing as they followed Buddha and his disciples along the road. At length Buddha, leaving the Kuru country, came to the kingdom of Sravastî, and there rested in the Jetavana vihâra. At this time, all the Bhikshus being assembled in the preaching-hall called Kia-li-lo, they said, 'It is wonderful, it is unprecedented,' &c." And then the Sûtra, following on the same lines as the Pāli, shows how Buddha entered the hall where the priests were and exhibits in succession the character of the sixty-two heretical views held respecting the existence of "soul" that is, a personal self, residing in the senses.

Now, the opening of the Pāli Suttá is this:—"Thus I heard. At one time Bhagavâ entered the high road between Râjagaha and Nalanda,

[1] Catalogue, Miscellaneous, Case 67.

attended by about 500 of his principal priests. The Paribbajako Suppiyo also entered the high road between Râjagaha and Nalanda, accompanied by his attendant pupil, the youth Brahmadatta: at which time the Paribbajako Suppiyo spake in many respects against Buddha—spake against his doctrines, and spake against the priesthood; while the youth, Brahmadatta, the attendant pupil of the Paribbajako Suppiyo, in many respects spake in favour of Buddha—spake in favour of his doctrines, and spake in favour of his priesthood: thus both the preceptor and pupil, engaged in the disputation which had arisen between them, continued following Buddha and the priests. At length Bhagavâ, accompanied by his priests, entered a royal residence at Amballaṭṭhika to pass the night," &c. The Pāli Sutta then goes on to relate how Buddha, entering the hall where the priests were assembled, questioned them as to the subject of their conversation, and from their answer takes occasion to exhibit his doctrine in reference to the non-existence of soul, just as we find him doing in the Chinese version of the Sûtra.

It is plain, as well from their agreements as from the slight differences that occur throughout, that these discourses are derived from one source, not the original, but from versions made from the original; and from one of these versions the Chinese translation was prepared. It will be an advantage when the entire Chinese Sûtra is before us in an English form; but there are difficulties in the way, which must be removed before that can be the case. But, from a perusal of the Chinese text, and a comparison with the English version from the Pāli, it is plain the two Sûtras are one and the same: and what is true in this case is also so in others. There is, for example, the well-known Sutta found in the southern canon, and called the "Mahâ-parinibbâna-Sutta," or "The Book of the Great Decease," a translation of which into English is found in the "Sacred Books of the East."[1] In his introduction, Dr. Rhys Davids speaks of some Chinese works bearing the same name as that of the Sutta he translates. All he states is very true: there are, in the Chinese collection, several books called Mahâparinirvâṇa Sûtras, and they are quite unlike the Pāli Sutta of that name. This only shows that in years following the *rédaction* of the early canon there were forgeries in the Buddhist society, as there have been in other cases. But there is one Chinese book to which Dr. Davids refers (p. xxxviii. *op. cit.*), which, on examination, turns out to be a version of the southern work, or, rather, a version of a collateral text existing in some part of India, and derived from the same source as the Pāli, which agrees in a remarkable way with the southern Sutta. It is called "Fo-pan-ni-pan-king," *i.e.*, the Parinirvāna of Buddha. It was translated into Chinese by a priest called Pih-fă-tsu, who was "devoted to the study of the sacred books, and was in the habit of reciting daily eight or nine thousand words." This last statement (and it frequently occurs in relation to other priests) shows us how these texts of the Buddhists were preserved, especially in the case of travelling priests,

[1] Vol xi.

who would, instead of carrying books with them, recite by word of mouth the texts they had committed to memory. This priest, who came to China about A.D. 300, translated the Sûtra in question; and, on examination, it is found that out of 324 sections in the Pāli there are only 46 wanting in the Chinese, and if from these 46 we deduct those sections which have evidently been interpolated in the Pāli, viz., from section 21 to section 42, we find that there are only 25 sections found in the Chinese version which do not occur in the southern work. These books, therefore, represent one original; and we are sure that the book Pih-fă-tsu brought to China, was a copy of, or a parallel text with, the Pāli Sutta now translated into English.

This argument might be followed up by reference to several other Sûtras, such as the Dhammachakka-ppavattana Sutta, the Sigalovada Sutta, the Dhammapada, and others, but it cannot be pursued further in this place. Sufficient has been said on the point to show that, as regards this section of the sacred books, the Buddhism of China is one in origin with that of the southern Buddhism of Ceylon.

§ 6. With respect to the third portion of the threefold collection or Tripiṭaka, which is known as the Abhidharma or metaphysics, so little is known by translation either from the north or south, that no comparison can be instituted. But from what we do know, it would appear that the northern school possesses a collection of works under this head, unknown elsewhere. I refer to the books called Prajña Pâramitâ, which are named by Mr. Hodgson as taking a conspicuous place in the Nepalese collection, and which occupy a similar place in China. The wearisome length to which these treatises run, and the constant repetition of the same idea, or verbal formula, will prevent any one from translating them; but from what we know of them, it is plain they cannot belong to the early school or have formed a part of the original collection of books. Their aim is to prove that all around us, *i.e.*, all phenomenal existence, is "empty" or "unreal"; that "the thing" is only "a name," and therefore cannot be treated as a reality. Whether there lies behind this complete negation the inference of a reality or positive existence that admits of no name *because* of its actual existence is a question not to be discussed, since there are no data before us; but, in any case, the teaching of the treatises classed under this name of Prajña Pâramitâ (that is, transcendental wisdom) is negative in its aim, and would appear to be the despair of reason in the search after the Infinite Being of God. These works are unknown in the south. They represent the Abhidharma class of books in Nepal, they occupy a similar place in the Chinese collection; but they are evidently late compilations, and can claim no consideration in the examination of the genuine division of the sacred books. Referring to the books named by Dr. Rh. Davids[1] under the head of Abhidamma, according to the southern school, there is no corresponding list, so far as is known, in the Chinese Tripiṭaka. It is probable

[1] "Buddhism," p. 21.

that when translated we may recognise some of them under different names in the Chinese collection; but, as far as our knowledge goes at present, there is here no correspondence; but in fact, beyond the Prajña Pâramitâ books, there is a large collection of Chinese works classed as Abhidharma, confessedly of a late origin. These are treatises (*S*âstras) written by men of distinction in the Buddhist community during various periods and for different aims and purposes. Now, all these, though classed as Abhidharma, are interpolations or intrusions into the primitive canon. They represent the scholastic period of the development of Buddhism, and can claim no original, or what we should call, canonical, authority, they are, therefore, not known elsewhere. They have been preserved principally under the form of Chinese translations, and they contain valuable data for the study of the system as a whole, but they have no authority as being "Tathâgatena vutto," *i.e.*, spoken by Buddha. Nevertheless, they are valuable works for a history of Buddhism, and the study of these books will become a necessity when we come to a searching investigation of the whole question.

Referring to the list of books in the Chinese Tripiṭaka,[1] it will be seen that there are 173 volumes (*han*) of Abhidharma works in that collection: seventy-three belonging to the "Little Vehicle" and fifty to the "Great Vehicle"; this will show at least the important place which they occupy in the north. With respect to their contents, they may be said to

[1] "Catalogue," pp. 3, 4.

be controversial in their character, taking generally a text from the canon and dilating upon it to prove a point in connexion with the belief of the writer or composer. Thus, in a work by Nâgârjuna, called the "*S*âstra of one *S*lóka," he takes a verse from an ancient and authentic book, and deduces from it a conclusion agreeable to his own views, as in this case for instance, that there is no such thing as self-nature. So also in another *S*âstra by the same writer, viz., the "Pranya mula śâstra tika," he labours to prove that Nirvāna is neither a positive condition of enjoyment, nor yet, on the other hand, the absence of existence.

"That which is not striven for nor 'obtained.'

"That which does not admit of limitation as to time, nor yet can be spoken of as 'eternal,'

"That which has no beginning, and does not come to an end,

"This is what is called Nirvāna."

And so the discourse proceeds through a succession of antithetical verses to show that Nirvāna, whilst it is not capable of definition, still "exists." Now, all this is peculiar to the north; it is the development of the early teaching of the system, and in that aspect it is valuable.

§ 7. There is one other aspect in which to regard the Buddhism of China and compare it with that of the southern school,—I mean as to external ritual; but here our knowledge is imperfect. We only know that, in general, the life of the Bhikshus in both cases is alike. The robes, vows, and discipline are in their main features identical; only in the point of worship, or what might be called liturgical service, do they differ. The objects of reverence in the north have been introduced at a later period, and especially in reference to Kwan-yin and Amitābha (and these form the chief portion of the northern *cultus*) they are entirely unknown in Ceylon. We shall be called to consider these differences further on, but meanwhile the agreement in discipline and religious life is sufficient to settle the point as to origin. The Chinese Buddhists derived their knowledge on these points from the same sources as the Buddhists of the south, and the two schools, so far, are but offshoots of one primitive stock. We have dwelt on this point at some length, because it was essential, *in limine*, to show that the Buddhism of which we speak is, in fact, not Chinese Buddhism but the Buddhism of India in China.

This will be plainer still from a brief notice of the historical connexion which can be traced between China and India previous to and after the introduction of Buddhism into the former country.

CHAPTER IV.

HISTORICAL CONNEXION BETWEEN INDIA AND CHINA.

§ 1. THERE is reason to believe that, from an early date, the tribes bordering on the north and west of the Chinese empire had moved in the direction of India and Western Asia, and, as they were able, had taken possession of the best and richest portion of the countries they invaded. The great Scythian invasion of Asia in the seventh century B.C. may have had its origin in the far East, caused by the pressure of nomadic tribes on the borders of the settled districts of Central Asia, and resulting in a general displacement, the Cimmerans being driven before the Scythian invaders, whilst they, on their part, were probably pressed on the east by restless tribes who sought larger pastures or richer settlements. However this may be, we find that a tribe of the Yue-chi, or White Huns, had moved away from the Chinese frontier so early as the second century B.C., and, according to Chinese accounts, had taken possession of the north-west provinces of India. Ma-twan-lin, the Chinese historian, tells us that at this time, *i.e.*, in the time of Wu-Ti, the emperor (B.C. 126), all these kingdoms, viz., of north-west India, belonged to the Yue-chi (Book cccxxxviii., fol. 2).[1] It was at this period that Wu-Ti, having

[1] *Vide* "Indian Antiquary," January, 1880, p. 16.

broken the power of the Hiung-nû, *i.e.*, the Kara-Nirus, sent an ambassador, called Chang-k'ien, to try and open communication with these Yue-chi, who were occupying the territory now called Tokharistan, whilst some of them had crossed the Indian frontier and penetrated as far as the valley of the Ganges, where they occupied some chief towns and were known as the Samvijjis or "united Yue-chis." They had established, in fact, a republican form of government in the very centre of Indian civilisation, and were destined to act an important part in the history of Buddhism and its diffusion through the north. The adventures of the ambassador, Chang-k'ien, are very remarkable, and as it was at this time that the first authentic communication of China with India took place, we will dwell on the point. The ambassador, Chang-k'ien, on his outward journey from China on his way to the Yue-chi, was captured by the Turks, *i.e.*, the Hiung-nû or Kara-nirus, who had driven the Yue-chi from the Chinese western frontier. He was held in captivity by them during ten years. Having at length escaped, he determined to carry out his mission to the Yue-chi, who dwelt to the north of the Oxus, where they had settled, after defeating the Tochâri, whom they had driven southward towards the Indian frontier. After travelling westward he came to Ta-wan, a country, according to our latest[1] authority, situated near Yarkand, to the east of the Pamir plateau. Here he tried to engage the inhabitants to enter into a league with the Chinese against the Hiung-

[1] Kingsmill.

nû or Turks (they were, in fact, the nomadic tribes who had wandered from the banks of the Selenga river to the north of the Gobi desert[1]), but without success. Thence he still went westward till he came to the country of the Yue-chi, but was unsuccessful with them also, for although they hated the Turks who had driven them out of Kansuh (Western China), still they feared them too much to enter into an alliance with so distant a power as China for offensive operations against them. Chang-k'ien then proceeded southwards to the country of Tahia (*i.e.*, of the Tochâri) intending to return to China through Tibet. Here he was again held in captivity for more than a year, but at length he once more escaped, and returned to China B.C. 126, after an absence of thirteen years. It was when Chang-k'ien was in Tahia that he had observed some Chinese goods and inquired how they came there. He then found out that they had come from the province of Sze-chuen, by way of India. No doubt this was an old trade-route from China, through Kamarupa, *i.e.*, the western part of Assam, towards the Ganges, and thence either to the central or northern provinces. Hiouen Thsang, one of the Chinese pilgrims,[2] when in the province of Kamarupa inquired as to the distance, and he found that a journey of two months was required "before reaching the country of Chou," *i.e.*, Sze-chuen. Chang-k'ien, therefore, advised the emperor to try to open the route for trade and military expeditions by this road towards Ta-wan, as he had heard

[1] "Handbook of the Chinese Language," by Doolittle, vol. ii., p. 206.

[2] Jul. ii., 81.

that the people of this last country had already entered into alliance with Tochâria and Parthia. The emperor was pleased, and accordingly directed Chang-k'ien to despatch expeditions from Sze-chuen along the four roads leading outwards from that province towards the west. Two of these expeditions, viz., those by the northern and southern routes, were stopped and defeated by the barbarians. They heard, however, of a country to the westward called Tin-yuet, where elephant-carriages were used, and the people of which carried on a clandestine trade with China. Chang-k'ien, therefore, determined to try to communicate with India (Tinyût) by opening a road in the direction of the south-west. This route would have passed through the territory of the "I," or western barbarians. Much money was spent in the attempt, but it was unsuccessful and finally given up. Chang-k'ien, however, affirmed that it was possible by this route to reach Tochâria, and a second time he tried negotiations with the "I"; but, being called away to conduct a force against the Hiung-nû, the undertaking appears to have failed. Without following the history of Chang-k'ien further, we can see, from what has been stated, the importance of events now happening with respect to China and its communications with the west,—for these occurrences ultimately led to an embassy from China to Parthia, probably during the reign of Mithridates II., B.C. 124, and to subsequent relationships between these two empires. We read, that when the Chinese envoy arrived in Parthia the king despatched a general with 20,000 horse to meet him on the eastern frontier, from which to the capital was about 1,000 li.[1] On the way they passed some ten cities; the inhabitants were all of the same race, and very numerous. On the return of the mission, he sent envoys with it that they might see the extent and power of China. "He sent with them eggs and the great bird of the country, and a curiously deformed man from Samarkand." Here we have a striking illustration of the kind of presents sent by Pandion (Porus), who reigned over some part of Western India, and might himself have been an Indo-Scyth, to Augustus. Among these gifts were a partridge larger than a vulture, large vipers and snakes, a tortoise-shell three cubits in length, and a deformed man without arms (a Hermes) who shot arrows with his feet.[2] These ambassadors were seen at Antioch by Nicolas of Damascus, who says there were only three who survived, and that they had a letter written in Greek on prepared skin, written by Porus, who said that he ruled over 600 kings, but that he valued much the friendship of Cæsar, and that he was ready in any way to open communications with him; and then Strabo adds, with reference to the deformed man, "whom we also have seen," giving reality to the narrative.[3] Let us remember that the ascetic who burnt himself at Athens also accompanied this embassy, over whom was raised the tomb with the inscription, "Here lies the Indian Sarmanacharya [one who leads the life of a Sarman or Shaman, *i.e.*, an ascetic] from Bargoza [Baroche], who, according to the custom of his native country, put an end to his life." It has been well

[1] Six li = 1 mile.

[2] Kingsmill.

[3] "Ον *καὶ ἡμεῖς εἴδομεν*, Strabo, xv., 719.

supposed that it was this very inscription which prompted the memorable words of St. Paul: "Though I give my body to be burned and have not charity, it profiteth me nothing."[1] All this, taken in connexion with the incidents occurring about the same time between China and the Indo-Scyths and Parthia, tends to show that a communication was being opened between the east and west which, if properly employed, might have led to a still closer acquaintance and ultimate friendship.

§ 2. In any case, it seems that it was by this acquaintance with the west that China first heard of Buddha and his doctrine. For Chang-k'ien reported to the emperor that "he had been told that in India they worshipped a divine person, Feou-to [Buddha]"; and another general, Hu Kiu-ping, saw at Hiu-to (a small district in the Pamir) "a golden image of the same person, which the king of that country adored." This is the first authentic record concerning a knowledge of Buddha in China. There are other statements made, indeed, in various books, with the view to make this knowledge date from an earlier period. For example, in a work written by Fa-lin, called the "Po-tse-lun," the writer brings a mass of evidence to show that Buddhist books were known in China before the time of the Emperor She-hwang-ti (B.C. 221). It was this monarch who built the great wall to check the incursions of the wandering tribes that threatened the empire; he also burnt the sacred books of Confucius, and assumed

[1] Bishop Lightfoot, "Colossians and Philemon," p. 395, n.

the title of the "first" emperor. The writer, Fa-lin, states that amongst the books burnt were the Buddhist Scriptures; but of this there is no proof, and, in fact, it is doubtful whether the Buddhist doctrine was at this time collected in a written form even in India, and there is no account of any translation made in China from any Indian original. We must regard this story as untrustworthy, and as part of the method followed by the contending sects in China who desired to claim priority in point of time for their religious founder. There is another story, also found in the pages of Fa-lin, equally improbable, relating to Li-fang, who is described as an Indian priest who came with seventeen companions to China in the reign of She-hwang-ti, and introduced the sacred writings of the Buddhist faith there. The emperor, it is said, shut them up in prison. During the night six men of supernatural character came and opened the prison doors and brought them out. On this, the emperor paid them reverence.[1] But, as Mr. Mayers observes, "the legend appears to have no historical basis." There are other notices equally fabulous to be found in Chinese books. We can, however, only accept as historical the circumstances above related in connexion with the Emperor Wu-ti, of the Han dynasty (B.C. 140–86), and the negotiations carried on by Chang-k'ien with the western tribes (especially with Mithridates II., King of Parthia, and with the Yue-chi), through which a knowledge of Buddha and his golden statue was brought to the ears of the

[1] "Chinese Readers' Manual," p. 114.

court and the Chinese people. At best we know little respecting the commotions of China and the restless tribes on its frontiers during the period to which we have referred. Until the pages of the Chinese historian, Sze-ma T'sien, have been carefully translated, and compared with statements found in Strabo and other historical works, our acquaintance with these events will remain imperfect. But yet, for a general outline, we know enough, and for convenience sake it may be thus summed up:—The tribes of nomads who threatened the western and north-western portions of China at the time of She-hwang-ti, 221 B.C., were turned, by the erection of the great wall, to seek an opening for their warlike tastes elsewhere. A portion of these tribes, called by the Chinese, Yue-chi, had been driven away from the western province of Kansuh by a horde of new invaders called Hiung-nû. These last were Turks, and became a terror to the empire: the energy and ability of the emperor Wu-ti (140–86 B.C.) broke their power; but the consequence of the pressure they exercised on the Yue-chi, who are described as fair-complexioned men (pink and white), and as being famous horsemen, and accustomed to dress in bright-coloured garments, caused them to encroach on the Tochâri, who had just broken up the Greek Bactrian kingdom. They drove out the Sâkas, or Sus, from the borders of the Pamir and its eastern slopes, and settled there. But in their early migration a portion of them, the Little Yue-chi, Ephthalitæ or White Huns, had already entered Tibet, and penetrated into North India and the Panjāb. We find them at Vaisâli and other towns bordering on the Ganges valley at an early date (probably as early as the middle of the second century B.C.); the others remained stationary on the north bank of the Oxus. Gradually they separated into lesser tribes and pushed further west, where, in all probability, they became known as Goths. The remaining portions finally coalesced, after the dismemberment of the Hiung-nû confederation by the Chinese, and a few years before the Christian era they marched in a body, led by the chief of the Gushan horde, to invade India and the entire Indian frontier. This was accomplished, and at the time of Kanishka, who reigned at, or shortly after, the beginning of our era, the whole of North India and the portions of Central Asia between Parthia and China were brought under their power. It is this Kanishka who became a Buddhist, and who built the vast towers and Topes (*stûpas*) which still remain in a ruined state, but yet monuments of his energy and zeal, throughout portions of Afghanistan and Cashmere. Thus it was the northern tribes of barbarians, as we call them, are seen to play a conspicuous part in the history of the early dissemination of the Buddhist doctrine, for it was through them that the first knowledge of Buddha reached China; and it is, as we shall now proceed to show, principally through them, and their zeal in spreading the knowledge of their books, that the system of Buddhism came eventually to be patronised and established in that empire.

CHAPTER V.

THE DREAM OF MING-TI.

§ 1. It was in the reign of the Chinese Emperor Ming-ti—who came to the throne A.D. 58, and reigned until A.D. 76—that Buddhism was definitely introduced into the empire. The capital at this time was at Loyang, the present Honan-fu; and it was here that for many years afterwards the great Buddhist centre of work lay. The Emperor Ming-ti had probably heard of the progress of Buddhism among the tribes bordering on China and India; and if, so early as the reign of Wu-ti, a golden image of the Indian saint had been set up in one of the small states bordering on the Chinese possessions, we may suppose with reason that the worship had spread in the interval, and some reports respecting the religion of Buddha come to the ears of the Chinese people. The emperor, at any rate, is said to have had a dream in the third year of his reign (A.D. 61) in which he saw a golden figure flying from heaven and hovering over his palace. Its head was surrounded by a glory equal to that of the sun and moon. Being moved by his dream to inquire about its meaning, one of his ministers, Fu-yih, told him that he had heard there was a divine person born in the west, called Buddha, and that probably his dream was connected with that circumstance. This clearly shows that Fu-yih had received some intelligence about this religion, and we might venture to think that he himself had a partial belief in the truth of what he had learned. But, at any rate, the emperor was induced, on hearing the minister's report, to send a mission to India in search of books or correct tidings about this mysterious personage. We are told in the annals, that the mission, numbering in all eighteen men, arrived in India and came as far as the country of the Yue-chi. It is probable that the district referred to under this name was the country of the Vajjis, or Vrijjis, who were in all probability an offshoot of the northern tribe of the Yue-chi, or White Huns, of whom we have already spoken. We are told by Sze-ma, that the languages spoken throughout the district where these tribes of northern people lived, from Ta-wan, *i.e.*, about Yarkand, as far west as Parthia, differed but slightly and were mutually intelligible. It would be easy, therefore, for the Chinese mission to proceed through these territories and pursue their inquiries respecting Buddha; and the special occurrences of the period would make their mission still more practicable, for at this time, probably, Kanishka was rising in power and his hordes preparing to invade India. They actually advanced as far as Magadha, south of the Ganges, and carried off from that country some of the sacred relics which were treasured there, as well as the persons of some eminent Buddhist teachers. At such a time, therefore, as this, the Chinese embassy penetrated to India and arrived among these Yue-chi. Here they collected books and pictures and relics, and, accompanied by two priests of the religion, they returned homewards and arrived at the capital, Loyang, A.D. 67. The emperor appears to have lent a ready ear to the instruction of the foreigners, and in the end caused a temple to be built in which the books and relics might be stored. The temple was called after the name of the "white horse" on which the books, &c., had been brought from the west. Such is the account given of the introduction of Buddhism into China: there is nothing improbable in the narrative, so far as the outline is concerned; and it is accepted on every hand by the Chinese themselves. But, as in most cases, there is much incredible matter added to the story—as for instance, with regard to the controversy between the Taouist priests and the new missionaries or envoys from India. In this account, we are assured that miracles were wrought to convince the emperor and people of the superior claims of the Buddhist religion; and it is added, the Taouist priests, abashed at their defeat, fell dead in the presence of the assembled multitudes. Leaving these stories out of the account, we seem to have before us a simple narrative of an event probable in itself, viz., of the introduction into China of books and teachers related to a foreign religion, now gathering notice throughout the east, and which had already spread to the confines of the empire. When we remember, too, that Kanishka and his followers had embraced this creed, and that it had probably found its way into Parthia,—all this taken into connexion with the story of the emperor's dream, makes it likely that we have in the foregoing record an historical fact, viz., that Buddhism found its way from India to China in 71 A.D.

CHAPTER VI.

THE ORIGIN OF THE SÂKYAS.

THE two Indian priests who accompanied the Chinese mission on its return to China were called Matanga and Gobharana (Chinese: Chu-fa-lan). They brought with them some books, and these they translated into Chinese. One of the books was "A Life of Buddha," in five chapters,—it is to this book we will now allude.

There is no life of Buddha known as a distinct work in the southern canon. But in China we find several such works. We shall consider some of them hereafter; for the present, there is one point that calls for notice, viz., the origin of the family to which Buddha belonged. The general name by which Buddha is known in the books is Sâkyamuni, or, the monk of the family of Sâkya. This name is not so common in southern accounts. Professor Childers[1] makes the following remarks:—"The Sâkyas formed a great clan or people engaged in agriculture, among whom probably a very few families were princely. Their territory appears to have been of some extent. Sâkyamuni, the Sâkya sage, or philosopher, is given as an epithet of Gautama (*i.e.*, Buddha). But I enter

[1] "Pāli Dictionary," *sub* Sākiyo. As a Sanscrit word it should be written Shâkya, or *S*âkya.

my protest against the continental custom of speaking of Gautama Buddha as Sâkyamuni, which is a mere epithet. Gautama is the name by which he is universally known and addressed." Perhaps nothing could show more clearly the difference that exists in the two schools of Buddhism than this remark. The northern tribes adopted the term Sâkya as the right name of Buddha, probably because it is related to the name of a tribe akin to themselves. The Sâkai[1] play an important part in the history of central Asia. We shall show that the Buddhism of the north was certainly framed and fashioned during its development by legends and doctrines derived from outside influences; so that it seems likely the very name of Sâkya was applied as a distinctive name to Buddha, because it brought him and his teaching more closely into connexion with the current of northern traditions. The title of Gautama, on the contrary, which is essentially Indian, "borrowed by the Sâkyas" (after their settlement in India) "from one of the ancient Vedic bard-families,"[2] is almost unknown in the Chinese books. It does occur undoubtedly, but compared with the name of Sâkya (which name, indeed, forms the title of the Buddhist community[3] in China) very seldom, and never as a distinctive title for Buddha after his enlightenment. M. Burnouf has the following remark as to the origin of the name Gautama.[4] "He, *i.e.*, Sâkyamuni, retained in one of

[1] Σάκαι.

[2] Oldenberg, "Life of Buddha," p. 95.

[3] Shih-kiau or Shih-tseu.

[4] Introduction, p. 155 and n.

the names which he bore, a trace of the connexion, essentially religious, which attached his family to the Brahmanic caste. He called himself the *S*ramana Gautama, or the Gautamide ascetic, without doubt because Gautama was the name of the sacerdotal family of the military race of the Sâkyas, who, in the quality of Kshattriyas, had neither ancestor nor tutelary saint after the manner of the Brahmans, but who were able to take, as the law of India allows, the name of the ancient sage to whose race their spiritual director belonged." In a note to this passage the same writer adds: "The origin of this title [of Gautama, or the Gautamas] remains unknown, and the explanation I have offered is, after all, only a conjecture." This account of the matter appears very probable, as we know from other sources that, according to a well understood custom, the Râjas (*i.e.*, kings of the Kshattriya caste) were considered members of the gotras of their purohitas, and called themselves after the latter.[1] And so Oldenberg states of the three Buddhas preceding the present age, who belonged to the Kshattriya caste, "The gotta [gotra] is mentioned as something existing as a matter of course: they are all Kondaññas."[2] This gotra name, then, of Gautama was probably adopted by the Sâkyas because it was that of the purohita, or court teacher, adopted first by them after their settlement in the district of Kapila,[3] where we find them at the opening of their history as a settled people. But

[1] Dr. Bühler, "Bharhut Stûpa," p. 129.

[2] For the Gotama gotra, *vide* M. Müller, "Ancient Sanskrit Literature," p. 381.

[3] "Life of Buddha," p. 413.

this would recommend the name especially to Indian converts. They would adopt it naturally, and apply it to Buddha naturally as his correct title; not so, however, among the northern, non-Indian people; they would hold to the name which they considered to be derived from one of their own tribes or clans, and this, in fact, would greatly account for their early adoption of the teaching of the Sâkya saint, and explain the hold it took almost at once on the northern tribes of invaders. There is an incident in a life of Buddha written by A*s*vaghosha, about the beginning of the first century, which will illustrate the point before us. Buddha had just attained what he called "enlightenment," and therefore was now a Tathâgata, or inspired prophet. He is going to seek some ascetics who had remained by him during his penance, but had left him when he broke his fast. They are described as speaking thus together, when they saw him approach:—"Seeing from far Tathâgata approaching, sitting together and conversing, thus they spake: 'This Gautama, defiled by worldly indulgence, leaving the practice of austerities, now comes again to find us here; let us be careful not to rise in salutation, nor let us greet him when he comes, nor offer him the customary refreshments: because he has broken his first vow, he has no claim to hospitality.' Having spoken thus, and so agreed, each kept his seat, resolved and fixed. And now Tathâgata slowly approached, when, lo! these men, unconsciously against their vow, rose and invited him to take a seat: offering to take his robe and alms bowl; they begged to be allowed to wash his feet, and asked him what he more required: thus in everything attentive they honoured him and offered all to him as teacher. They did not cease, however, to address him still as Gautama, after his family.[1] Then spake the lord to them, 'Call me not after my familiar name, for it is a rude and careless way of speaking . . . call me, therefore, Buddha.'" Here we see the familiar name of Gautama is forbidden, and consequently it is seldom met with in the books found in China; but he is still called Sâkya and Sâkyamuni; and those who take the vows are frequently distinguished by the name, as distinctly religious, as for instance, Fa-hien, the pilgrim, is known as Shih Fa-hien, *i.e.*, the Buddhist priest, Fă-hien.

The origin of the term Sâkya is referred by the early writers to a story related of one of the ancestors of the family. We shall notice in the following section the story in its details. It will be sufficient now to mention that Ikshvâku Virudhaka, who reigned at Potala, on the Indus, had banished his four eldest sons from his kingdom, and afterwards, on inquiry, finding that they had established a powerful kingdom elsewhere and were reigning in prosperity, is said to have exclaimed, "They are able! they are able!" which, put into a Sanscrit form, was converted into this name Sâkya, from the root *sak*, "to be able." This is probably an invention; there may be a verbal root, indeed, found in other languages of the form here named, signifying "ability" or "power," and it is possible that the Sâkyas were a race remarkable for

[1] Asvaghosha's, "Life of Buddha," K. iii., *varga* 15, line 1,230.

their strength, and had derived their name from this characteristic, just as in other cases

"Pauci
Diis geniti, potuere,"

but there is no proof of it, and for the present we must be content to consider the Sâkyas as an old family found in North India of an exclusive and proud character, derived probably from an immigrant branch of the great Sâka race that from early time, according to Strabo, occupied the frontier land along the borders of all India.[1]

This may be gathered from a consideration of the circumstances mixed up with the Buddhist legend as it comes to us in the north. Whilst, on the one hand, there is no Brahman or native Indian family known by the name of Sâkya, on the other, there are several circumstances which tend to show that these people were allied to a northern, non-Indian race. They were a chivalrous, exclusive, and proud people. Their own legend connects them with a tribe or family settled at an early period at the mouth of the Indus; and, when they are found at Kapilavastu, it is still as emigrant settlers who had sought this spot so as to continue a distinct people, and, for the purpose of preserving their pure descent, intermarrying amongst themselves, brother with sister. But we may go further than this: the Sâkyas appear to have had the character not only of a distinct race or tribe, but a degree of sanctity or holiness is attached to them as a race. There is a curious story told by the

[1] Strabo, lib. xi., p. 513.

Chinese pilgrim, Hiouen Thsang, respecting them which may be given as an illustration of this.[1] He tells us that he saw, among many other remains, in the country of Kapilavastu, *i.e.*, the country over which the Sâkyas ruled, four little towers, or *stûpas*, and he goes on thus :—" This is the place where four Sâkya youths withstood an army. When first Prasenajita became king [of Kosala] he sought an alliance by marriage with the Sâkya race. The Sâkyas despised him as not being of their family, and so they gave him as his wife the daughter of a slave whom they largely endowed : but this they did to deceive him. The king made this girl his principal queen, and she bore him a son in due time, whom they called Virudhaka. This prince, when he grew up, desiring to complete his education, purposed to go to the country of his maternal uncle, *i.e.*, to the king of the Sâkyas, for this end. Having arrived at the south part of the city [of Kapilavastu], he there saw a new preaching-hall, and there he stopped his chariot. The Sâkyas, hearing of his arrival, went out and drove him away, saying : 'How dare you, base-born fellow ! occupy this abode, a hall built by the Sâkyas, intended for a preaching-hall for Buddha ?' So then, after Virudhaka had succeeded to the throne, he longed to revenge the insult he had received. Raising an army, therefore, he occupied the country with his troops, who took possession of the fields (and devastated the crops). Now, it happened that four men of the Sâkyas were engaged in ploughing between the water-

[1] Hiouen Thsang, Jul. II., 317–59.

courses in a particular field; seeing the soldiers approach, they opposed their progress, and eventually drove them off. After this, they entered the town and told what they had done. Then their clansmen, considering that their tribe was one in which a succession of holy kings had appeared, and in which the sacred king of religion had now been born (*i.e.*, Buddha), and that now these four men, notwithstanding this, had dared to act revengefully and cruelly, and to slay and kill, without patiently enduring wrong, and so had brought disgrace on their name, drove them from their home. Being thus banished, they went to the north of the Snowy Mountains, and became each one of them king of a different country. One ruled over the country of Bamian; another over Udyâna; another over Himatala; and another over Sâmbî [Kausâmbi ?]. Here they have reigned without interruption, transmitting their kingly authority from generation to generation." To this account, M. Stas. Julien (the first translator of Hiouen Thsang) appends the following note:—"It seems strange that these noble champions should be driven from their town and exiled by their parents because they resisted the troops of the destroyer of the great Sâkya family." And so it does appear strange; but the story confirms the supposition, which is in keeping with the entire Sâkya legend, that these people had traditions among them relating to the sanctity of their tribe and the appearance of a great saint amongst them, which explains a great deal of the Buddhist expanded history. With respect to the foregoing extract, the circumstance of the banishment of the Sâkyas is also found in the southern records, but the cause of it does not appear to be named. "When Buddha yet lived [so says the Atthakathâ, *i.e.*, the commentaries on the sacred books, belonging to the Uttaravihâro priests in Ceylon], driven by the misfortunes produced by the war of Prince Vidudhabo [Virudhaka], certain members of the Sâkya line, retreating to Himavanto, discovered a delightful and beautiful location, well watered, and situated in the midst of a forest of lofty bo and other trees. Influenced by the desire of settling there, they founded a town at a place where several great roads met, surrounded by durable ramparts, having gates of defence therein, &c. Moreover, that city having a row of buildings covered with tiles, which were arranged in the pattern of the plumage of a peacock's neck, and as it resounded with the notes of flocks of 'konchos' and 'mayuros' [peafowls], from this circumstance, these Sâkya lords of this town and their children and descendants were renowned throughout Jambudwipa by the title of Moriya. From that time the dynasty has been called the Moriyan dynasty."[1] This is probably without authority, but the record of the early dispersion of members of the Sâkya family in the region of the Himavanto is, to all appearance, a reliable one, as it is preserved in the south as well as the north. No doubt, then, these Sâkya youths not only settled in these districts because they found members of allied tribes already there, but, having established themselves there, they would perpetuate the traditions of their own

[1] M. Müller's "History of Ancient Sanskrit Literature," p. 285.

tribe and preserve the knowledge of the coming of a great teacher amongst their people. We do not wonder, therefore, to find the doctrine and discipline of Buddha so readily accepted at a subsequent period in these regions and by these tribes.

There is a curious confirmation of this idea of sacredness attached to the Sâkya tribe to be drawn from a remark found in Josephus. Before referring to it, however, it will be necessary to premise that the Sâkya family were known also as Ikshvâkus, or the "sugar-cane" family. This name was derived from the old king who reigned at Potala, on the Indus, who was called Ikshvâku Virudhaka. Doubtless, he inherited the name from his ancestors, or the clan to which he belonged. That the Sâkyas were known as Ikshvâkus (Pāli, Okkákas) is evident from all the records. "The son of Káláranjanaka was A*s*oka, whose successor was the first Okkáka king" (Spence Hardy, "M. B.," p. 130). And the last of this race was Amba or Okkáka III., from whom, in a direct line, descended the father of Buddha. The peculiar character for holiness or sanctity attaching to this family is to be gathered from various notices found scattered through the different lives of Buddha. For instance, we are told in the southern records, that when the four sons of the Okkáka king, after their banishment from Potala, consulted together as to their future home, they said, "We have so large a retinue that there is no city in Jambudwipa which could withstand us; but if we were to seize on any kingdom by force it would be unjust and contrary to the principles of the Okkáka race, it would be inconsistent in us to take that which belongs to another, we will therefore erect for ourselves a city and reign in righteousness." Again, the Chinese version of the "Buddhacharita, or Life of Buddha," by Asvaghosha (dating, as we have said, from the beginning of the first century, A.D.), begins in this way:—"Descended from the Ikshvâku family, pure in mind, of unspotted virtue, reverenced by all, was Sudohodana, the father of Buddha." And in other passages the Ikshvâkus are spoken of as distinguished for their purity and piety of life. It is curious to find in Josephus a passage which seems to refer to this "sugar-cane" family of India. It occurs in the fourth book "against Apion," § 22, p. 640.[1] The author is showing that the most eminent of the Greeks were acquainted with the Jewish nation. He says:—"For Clearchus, who was the scholar of Aristotle, and inferior to no one of the Peripatetics whomsoever, in his first book concerning sleep, says that 'Aristotle, his master, related what follows of a Jew,' and sets down Aristotle's own discourse with him. The account is this as written down by him:—'Now, for a great part of what this Jew said, it would be too long to recite it; but what includes in it both wonder and philosophy, it may not be amiss to discourse of. Now, that I may be plain with thee, Hyperochides, I shall herein seem to thee to relate wonders, and what will resemble dreams themselves.' Hereupon Hyperochides answered modestly, and said, 'For that very reason it is that all of us are very desirous of hearing what thou

[1] Whiston's translation.

art going to say.' Then replied Aristotle : 'For this cause it will be the best way to imitate that rule of the rhetoricians which requires us first to give an account of the man and of what nation he was, that so we may not contradict our master's directions.' Then said Hyperochides : 'Go on, if it please thee. 'This man,' then said Aristotle, 'was by birth a Jew, and came from Cœle-Syria ; these Jews are derived from the Indian philosophers ; they are named by the Indians, Calami, and by the Syrians, Judæi, and took their name from the country they inhabit.'" And then Josephus goes on to say, that "Aristotle discoursed particularly of the great and wonderful fortitude of this Jew in his diet and continent way of living." We cannot doubt that the word used by Aristotle, "Calami," is a translation of the Indian "Ikshvâkus," or the "sugar-cane" people. He speaks of them as philosophers, which is natural enough ; but he compares them with the Jews because of their purity and continency of life. There seems here to be a covert reference to the family from whom the Buddhists sprang, and perhaps to the Buddhists themselves, known as Ikshvâkus. It is true, that there were other families in India belonging to these Ikshvâkuidæ besides the race of the Sâkyas. The kings of Ayodhyâ were of this family,[1] and, according to Oldenberg,[2] the later ages trace back the royal race of Eastern Hindustan to Ikshvâku ; but this does not stand in the way of the unanimous tradition found in the Buddhist books with reference to the

[1] "Ancient Sanskrit Literature," p. 408.

[2] "Life of Buddha," p. 403.

pure descent of the founder of their religion,—"that he belonged to the holy family of the Okkákas, in which there had been a succession of sacred kings, known as Chakravartins." These Ikshvâkus were, from an early date, settled at Potala, and thence established themselves as a royal race at Ayodhyâ, and afterwards at Kapilavastu.[1]

If, then (in agreement with our supposition), the Sâkyas were an immigrant tribe settled in India, and related to the Sâkas, and if they were described as peculiar for their "just laws and righteous conduct," do we find anything corresponding with this description among the Sâkas themselves? We know little of them, but yet there are not wanting some references on this point which seem to sustain the argument. In the seventh Book of Strabo's "Geography" there is some discussion in reference to the character of the Getæ, amongst whom Zamolxis, the teacher of Pythagoras, was esteemed as a god. These nomads were remarkable for their justice, *δικαιότατοι ἀνθρώπων*. And he connects them with the blameless Æthiopians of Homer, who were, in fact, Scythians. The whole passage will be found p. 300. And then he proceeds to say that Æschylus also speaks of the Scythians as a just race (*εὔνομοι Σκύθαι*), and so he connects them with the Sacæ or Sâkas, quoting Chœrilus, *Μηλονόμοι τε Σάκαι γενεᾷ Σκύθαι*, of whom he says they were "*justa gens hominum.*" And so Homer, speaking of the Æthiopians, calls them "blameless." Were these Æthiopians a branch of the Sâkas? There is, in

[1] With respect to the "Calami," see note A.

Chinese, a well-known tribe of the Yue-chi (or Yue-ti), called Ye-tha, and the situation which Homer gives his eastern people, close to the flowings of ocean, would correspond with the mountains of Gandhâra, the "earth-holding mountains" of the Buddhist cosmogony. But, in any case, it would seem, from what has been said, that there was a belief prevalent from earliest times that a tribe of nomads, corresponding with the Sacæ, or Sâkas, were renowned for their justice and purity (blamelessness) of life, and that the same character is given to the Ikshvâkus, or Sâkyas, found as settlers in India, from whom the founder of Buddhism, the lion of the Sâkya tribe, sprang.

These remarks have been made with a view to clear the way for a conclusion to which the legend of Buddha seems to lead us. It will be seen that in the northern story of his life and teaching there are found fragments of early traditions which have been preserved in their integrity and completeness in the Jewish records. The argument, therefore, which the presence of such fragmentary allusion seems to suggest is this: that the Sâkya race, and perhaps other allied families or tribes, had preserved amongst them some broken knowledge derived from earliest time, and that this knowledge took shape in a distorted form in the legend of their founder. Many allusions seem to express what is called a "felt want" in their system. And as the knowledge of Buddha's teaching spread further and further north, so the system he had framed adapted and adopted these fragments of truth, until we have before us the entire legend as it is known now among northern nations. What this legendary story is we shall next proceed to inquire, only premising this much,—that it is the result of a succession of increments added on to one simple historical narrative, which narrative is found in the earliest records of the southern Pāli school.

CHAPTER VII.

THE LEGEND OF SÂKYA BUDDHA.

It is plain that, so far as our argument, stated in the previous section, is concerned, it does not matter whether the legend of Buddha's life as known in China be derived from the authentic books belonging to the southern canon or not. The legend took shape, and it must have derived its parts from either (1) the original story, or (2) from traditions known among the people where it gathered its present form. As we have it in China, it is a perfect whole. The Buddha descended from heaven, and he was incarnated miraculously; born in a royal line, he was impelled by a sense of the misery of the world to seek enlightenment in order to save the world; he was enlightened and became a teacher, gathered disciples around him, converted those that were to be saved, and died at the end of a long life, surrounded by his followers; and, finally, after his death, was honoured and worshipped, being still present in the world in the form of a bequeathed system of law (*dharmakâya*). Now, we find that a great portion of this is unknown in the south, or rather in the early books of the Pāli school. We are told that "no biography of Buddha has come down to us from ancient times, from the age of the Pāli texts, and we can safely say that no such biography was in existence then."[1] But, at any rate, so early as the beginning of our era, a life of Buddha in seven chapters was brought to China, and that this contained the full legendary story as it is now commonly known is evident from extracts found in works at present extant.[2] Beside this, however, is the life of Buddha by Asvaghosha, known as the "Buddha Charita Kâvya," which was undoubtedly written in the early part of the first century, and must have been founded on a legendary history in common circulation before it was put in a poetical form by that writer. We are brought to the conclusion, therefore, that between the period of the collection of Pāli books, which may perhaps be placed about 350 B.C. and the first century B.C., the legend as known in the north was framed, and so familiarly known that it was put into a poetical form by Asvaghosha, who flourished either just before or just after the Christian era. It has been said that the particulars of the legend are derived from nature-myths, and that these myths are to be found hidden in Indian texts. But the fault of this theory seems to lie here, that the legend of Buddha is not framed after any Indian model, but is to be found worked out, so to speak, among northern nations who were ignorant of, or indifferent to, any of the pedantic stories of the Brahmans. In the southern and primitive records, the terms of the legend are wanting. Buddha is not born of a royal family; he is not tempted before his

[1] Oldenberg, "Life of Buddha," p. 78.

[2] Especially the "Shih Shing taou," by Wong pûh.

enlightenment; he works no miracles; and he is not a universal saviour.[1] Whence come these ideas in the legend of the north? for we must repeat, the legend is known nowhere else in its completeness but in northern records or southern adaptations from northern records. It seems far-fetched to suppose that the northern tribes had recourse to the figurative and obscure readings of the Brahmanas and the epics of India, and there can be no proof brought to show that the traditions found elsewhere were known amongst the tribes who adopted Buddhism, except in the shape of a common inheritance. It is for the champion of the nature-myth theory to prove that the common folk-lore of the northern people was based on nature-myths only, and not on a common tradition. We have already indicated that such traditions might have existed among the holy or pious families of the far east, and from them have passed into the history of Buddha, the great sage of the Sâkya race.

We shall now briefly particularise the leading events in the legendary life of Buddha, as it is known in the early life written by Asvaghosha.

[1] Oldenberg, "Life of Buddha," *passim*.

CHAPTER VIII.

THE "LIFE OF BUDDHA," BY ASVAGHOSHA.

THIS writer was the eleventh patriarch, as it is called, of the Buddhist order. He was born in Middle India, of a Brahman family, and brought up in that faith; but, having been converted to Buddhism, he became an opponent of his old creed, and laboured earnestly to show its insufficiency. He was a poet and musician. It is said the early hymns of the Buddhists were chiefly written by him. He was taken from Magadha, in Middle India, to the north, by Kanishka, and it is probable he there wrote the life of Sâkya Buddha to which we are about to refer. In fixing the date of A*s*vaghosha, we have several notices to guide us, but the most satisfactory clue is the agreement in all the records that he was a contemporary of Kanishka. This monarch was an Indo-Scyth, who had come (*circ.* A.D. 70) to be the ruler of all North India, and probably of a great portion of Central Asia. There is no certainty as to the exact date of his reign, but it is now made probable that he was the founder of the *S*âka era or *samvat*, or that this era dates from his death. This would make him flourish in the middle of the first century A.D., and, therefore, A*s*vaghosha would probably be living from the early part of this century till towards the close of it. He would thus be contemporary with the rise and establishment of the Christian religion in Western Asia. At any rate, it is sufficiently clear that A*s*vaghosha, in writing a life of Buddha, derived his material from India and its neighbourhood, and that we have in his book a purely independent composition. We do not know whether the life of Buddha taken to China A.D. 72 was in any way derived from this work of A*s*vaghosha, or whether he derived his material from this work; but it is likely that the envoys sent by Ming-ti would hear of the writings of the patriarch of the Northern Buddhists, and it is possible that the book they took back with them was connected (either as the original form of it, or as a digest) with the "Buddha Charita Kâvya" (*i.e.*, the "Epic of Buddha").

The poem is in five *kiouen*, or chapters, divided into 28 sections (*vargas*). It embraces 2,310 *slókas*, or verses, of four lines each. Thus, in the Chinese version there are 9,240 lines. The outline of the biography, or the poetical romance, is this:—The miraculous conception of Buddha, by the descent of a spirit on his mother, Māyā. She was pure in mind as the water-lily, and strong and calm in her purpose as the earth. When the time for her delivery approached, she begged the king to allow her to visit a favourite garden called Lumbinî, and to wander therein, amid its fountains and its flowers and fruit-trees. Resting on a beautiful couch, religiously observing the rules of pure discipline, her son was miraculously born—constrained by great pity, come to deliver the world—

on the eighth day of the fourth month,—a season of serene and agreeable character. Without causing his mother pain, he came forth from her right side, sparkling with light, as when the sun rises from the east. He deliberately stood upright and took seven steps, planting his foot evenly on the ground as he went, and then looking to the four quarters, he spake thus: "Now only am I born this once for the purpose of saving all the world." Forthwith from heaven there fell two streams of pure water upon his head, and causing refreshment to his body. Meanwhile, the *devas* in space raised in responsive harmony their heavenly songs, whilst he is carried on a jewelled couch back to the palace. There the soothsayers cast his horoscope, "this most excellently-endowed child will bring deliverance to the entire world, none but a heavenly teacher has a body such as this ; or, if he be induced to continue in the world (that is, as a secular person), then he will become a universal monarch, mighty in his righteous government, ruling the world, uniting all other kings under his sway." Then another well-known seer, called Asita, comes to the palace, and, taking the child in his arms, predicts his greatness as a teacher and sage. "This son of thine," he said, addressing the father, "will rule the world; born for the sake of all that lives, he shall give up his royal estate, escape from the domain of sin (the five desires) with resolution and with diligence, practise austerities, and then, awakening, grasp the truth. The heavy gates of gloomy unbelief, fast kept by covetousness and lust, all living things confined within, he shall open, and give deliverance to all. Let the king, then, doubt not; nor in himself encourage thought of pain." The horoscope finished, the king distributes gifts to all within his kingdom, and when the child was ten days old, he takes him to a temple of the gods and offers sacrifice; then going back, the child is carefully brought up within the palace. The poem then relates how universal prosperity prevailed throughout the land. There was no biting hunger, the soldiers' weapons were at rest, all diseases disappeared; throughout the kingdom all the people were piously affectioned, they sought their daily profit righteously, and no covetous or money-loving spirit ruled them. All practised the four rules of purity, and every hateful thought was banished. So then, because of such propitious signs, the child was called Siddhârtha (perfection of all things). And now his mother dies, and goes to the heaven where the thirty-three gods rule. Precious gifts are offered by members of the tributary states, presents of various kinds,—oxen and sheep, deer, horses, chariots, precious vessels, elegant ornaments fit to please the prince's heart: but his mind was not disturbed by glittering baubles such as these. And now he was brought to learn the useful arts, when, lo! but once instructed, he excelled his teachers. His father, seeing his exceeding talent and his deep purpose to forsake the world, selected for the youth a wife, Ya*s*odharâ, majestic like the queen of heaven, constant ever, cheerful night and day, holding the palace pure and quiet, full of dignity and grace. So with such a wife and countless women as attendants on her, the prince lived in his palace. Then, as time went on, a son, Râhula, was born to them, on which the king, Suddhodana, was encouraged to believe that now his son would love his child and not forsake his home.

At length, the prince desires to leave his palace for a time to see the gardens. "Without are pleasant garden glades, pure refreshing lakes, and flowing fountains; every kind of flower and trees with fruit, arranged in rows, deep shade beneath." The prince desired, as a chained elephant longs for the desert wild, to visit these. The king accordingly takes the precaution to have the way prepared, to remove offensive matter, all persons old or sick, all who suffered grief or pain through poverty, these were all removed, so that his son might, in his present humour, see nothing to afflict his heart. But it was vain; a *deva* of the pure abodes assumed the form of an aged man and stood beside the path, "struggling for life, weak and oppressed." The prince, beholding him, inquired, "what kind of man is this?" The charioteer, embarrassed, scarcely dared to answer truly, till the *deva* "added his spiritual power," and caused him to frame a true reply, "This is an 'old man,'—he was once a sucking child, brought up and nourished at his mother's breast, and as a youth full of sportive life, handsome, and filled with enjoyment; as years passed on, his frame decaying, he is brought to feel the waste of age." On this, the prince greatly agitated, asks, "Is yonder man the only one bent down with age, or shall I be such as he, and others also?" The charioteer again replies, "Throughout the world, this is the common lot; the youthful form must wear the garb of age." Then the prince ordered his chariot to return, and "with speedy wheels take me to my palace." Reflecting there on the affliction of age, his mind seems to be ill at ease, and found no rest in anything within his home. After this, to alleviate his sorrow, the king arranges other excursions, but on each occasion another painful sight is brought before him by the *deva* :—first a sick man, "his body swollen and disfigured, sighing with deep-drawn groans, his hands and knees contracted, his tears flowing piteously." The prince again puts the question, "What sort of man is this?" and on receiving a reply similar to the former, he once more goes back to meditate. On the third excursion, he beholds a dead man carried to the grave; "four persons carrying a corpse lifted on high appeared before the prince; the surrounding people saw it not, but only the charioteer and he; "What is this they carry?" said the prince. And now the gods constrained the charioteer to answer thus: "This is a dead man, all his power of body gone, life departed; his heart deprived of thought; his intellect dispersed; his spirit fled; his body withered and decayed, stretched out as a dumb log; family ties snapped; all his friends who loved him once, clad in white cerements, desiring to behold him not, are taking him to lie within the tomb." Then the prince, hearing the word DEATH, bent down his body on the chariot leaning-board, and stammered forth, with bated breath and struggling accents: "O worldly men! how fatally deluded! beholding everywhere the body turned to dust, yet living more carelessly." Then he went back again to meditate.

After these painful sights, the prince is taken, by way of diversion, to see a ploughing match; but when he saw the ploughmen plodding along the furrows, and the writhing worms, his heart again was moved with piteous feeling, and anguish pierced his soul to see the labourers at their toil, struggling with painful work,—their bodies bent, their hair dishevelled, the dripping sweat upon their faces, their persons fouled with mud and dust; the ploughing oxen, too, bent by the yokes, their lolling tongues and gaping mouths. "The nature of the prince, loving, compassionate, his mind conceived most poignant sorrow, and, nobly moved to sympathy, he groaned with pain." He then retires to a solitary spot, and, seated beneath a flowering Jambu tree, he gives himself to deepest thought. He is represented as then, for the first time, entering the mysterious condition of rapt ecstacy so frequently alluded to in Buddhist books, and called Dhyāna, or Samādhi. It may, perhaps, be as well to quote the words of the poem itself on this point. "Lost in tranquil contemplation, he reflected that youth, vigour, strength of life, constantly renewed without long stay, in the end fulfilled the rule of ultimate destruction." This was the subject of his meditation: then, "without excessive joy or grief, without confusion, and with no hesitation in his thoughts, without dull dreaminess or excited longing, without aversion or discontent, but perfectly at peace, without impediment, radiant with the beams of gathering illumination—thus he sat."[1] Whilst meditating

[1] See Fig. 1, plate xxv., "Tree and Serpent Worship."

thus, a *deva* of the pure abode, transformed into a Shaman, or religious ascetic, came to the place. The prince, with due consideration, rose to meet him, and inquired respecting him "who he was." In reply he said, "I am a Shaman. Depressed and sad at thought of age, disease, and death, I have left my home to seek some way of rescue, but everywhere I find old age, disease, and death: all things hasten to decay; no permanency is there anywhere. Therefore," he goes on, "I search for the happiness to be found in that which never perishes, that never knew beginning, that looks with equal mind on enemy and friend, that heeds not wealth nor beauty; the happiness to be found in solitude, in some lone dell, free from molestation, all thoughts about the world destroyed." And having spoken thus he disappeared. This was the turning-point of the prince's history. From this time the idea of Nirvāna deepened and widened in him. "His body as a peak of the golden mountain, his shoulder like the elephant's, his voice like the spring thunder, his deep blue eye like that of the king of oxen, his mind full of religious thoughts, his face bright as the full moon, his step like that of the lion king,—thus he entered in the palace, and straightway sought his father's presence. Then he explained his dread of age, disease, and death, and sought respectfully permission to become a hermit." We need not dwell on the account of his further struggle against a sense of duty or affection for his father. The culminating scene is when he awoke in the middle of the night and saw the sickly lamps, and the confusion of the music-and-dancing women as they slept upon the floor. "Now," he exclaimed, "I have awakened to the truth; resolved am I to leave such false society!" He forthwith summoned his equerry to bring his horse, and, notwithstanding all his protests, brought him to comply. "Forthwith, on that eventful night, he left the palace gates," the man streaming with light, the outcome of his high resolve; the horse like the white floating cloud. "Thus man and horse, both strong of heart, went onwards, lost to sight like streaming stars; but ere the eastern heavens flashed with the light of morn they had advanced three *yojanas*."

The prince forthwith dismisses his equerry and his horse. He sends back his jewelled turban, cuts off his hair, and assumes the brown robe of a hermit. After vainly seeking satisfaction in the company of some pain-practising ascetics, he resolves to seek wisdom for himself. Accordingly, he repairs to a quiet spot by the banks of a river called the Nairanjana, not far from the little town of Gayâ, and there for six years practised the most severe penance,—each day, the legend says, "eating one hemp grain—his body shrunk and attenuated, his limbs exceeding weak, his heart of wisdom increasing more and more." At length he arrived at the conviction that these were not the means to extinguish desire and produce ecstatic contemplation (Dhyāna). He resolved, therefore, to refresh his members, and cause his mind to rest by partaking of food in moderation. He rose and bathed in the Nairanjana, but so weak was he that scarcely, with the help of a bending branch, he could mount the river bank. At this time, a shepherd's daughter, called Nandâ, was apprised by a *deva* of the opportunity she had of being the first to offer food to the Bodhisattva. She came forthwith, "upon her wrists the bracelets of chalcedony contrasted with her robes of blue, as colours of the rounded river bubble." She reverently offered him some rice-milk, sweet and perfumed. On eating it, he felt his strength come back afresh; and then, leaving the spot of painful penance, he wandered on alone towards the tree beneath which he hoped to reach perfect enlightenment. This tree, commonly known as the Bodhi tree, or tree of knowledge, was near at hand; and as he went, the legend says, the earth was shaken, and the rumbling of the earthquake heard. Various signs presented themselves, and, accompanied by *devas* and gazed on by *nâgas*, he came and took his seat, "with upright body, feet placed under him, not carelessly arranged, but with his limbs all firmly fixed and compact." Thus he sat, "nor shall he rise again," the *nâga* cried, "until his undertaking is completed."

This is the culminating point of the legend, and it is surrounded therefore with strange concomitants. We are told that Māra, the lord of the world of sense —that is, of sensuous indulgence—"enemy of religion, foe of those who seek deliverance [from sin], and therefore rightly called 'the wicked'"[1]—he alone was grieved, and sent his daughters to attempt to allure the princely hermit from his purpose. In vain they try their arts. Then Māra comes himself, and thus

Pisuna.

addresses the prince, "Rise up! begone!" and points his poisoned arrow at him. Equally in vain, for "the Bodhisattva's heart remains unmoved: he felt no doubt, no fear." Then the scene changes, and Māra calls his army host, "of horrid shapes and monstrous forms," to attack his enemy. Some holding spears, some grasping trees, others wielding ponderous maces, with shapes and bodies terrible: thus the wicked goblin troop gathered round the tree, intent on tearing limb by limb the Bodhisattva's body. From the four sides the flames burst forth, and fiery steam ascended up to heaven; tempestuous winds arose on every side; the mountain forests shook and quaked; wind, fire, steam, and dust combined, produced a pitchy darkness, rendering all invisible. But still the Bodhisattva, "silent and quiet in the midst remained, his face, unchanged, as calm as heretofore, like the great lion king placed amongst all the beasts howling and growling round him; so he sat, a sight unseen before, so strange and wonderful." At length Māra, wearied of his efforts, filled with fear, again took up his way to heaven [Māra's palace, as the lord of the world of pleasure, was in the heaven of "desire"], whilst all his host, "overwhelmed with grief and disappointment, fallen from their high estate, reft of their warrior pride, their warlike weapons and accoutrements thrown away—like as when some cruel chieftain slain, the hateful robber band is all dispersed—so Māra's army, disconcerted, fled away." Then comes the climax. "Bodhisattva now remained in peaceful quiet; the morning sunbeams brighten with the dawn; the dust-like mist, dispersing, disappears; the moon and stars pale their faint light; the barriers of the night are all removed; whilst from above a fall of heavenly flowers pay their sweet tribute to the Bodhisattva." Then, passing through successive stages of rapt ecstacy, he traces back all suffering to the one cause of ignorance (*avidya*), that is, absence of light, and then himself attains the great awakened state of "perfect light." Thus did he complete the end of "self"; as fire goes out for want of grass, thus he had done what he would have men do; he first had found the way of perfect knowledge, then, lustrous with all-wisdom, the great *rishi* sat, perfect in gifts, whilst one convulsive throe shook the wide earth. This is the condition of the Buddha, or the awakened, and by this name henceforth he is to be called. At first, so says the legend, Buddha was disinclined to preach or teach amongst men, for who would have the power to comprehend the truth; but he is represented as being urged by Brahmadeva not to entertain such thoughts. "Oh, let your loving heart be moved with pity towards the world burthened with vexing cares," such is his appeal. Then Buddha's heart relents, and "greatly was his pity nourished, and purposed was his mind to preach." Having received food from some merchantmen, he set out towards Benares, intending to find "the five men" who had for six years shared his fast, but had left him when he took the rice-milk from Nandâ. Step by step, like the king of beasts (the lion), did he advance towards the Kasi city, bent on this design, "to preach Nirvāna and convert the world." On his way, he meets a young Brahman called Upaka, who, struck with the appearance of the great Bhikshu (the great mendicant), stood with reverent mien beside the road. Having gazed upon him with astonishment, he asked him "of what noble tribe he was, and who his master." Buddha replies, "I have no master, no honourable tribe; but, self-taught in this profoundest doctrine, I have arrived at perfect wisdom." This wisdom he calls Sambodhi, or Sambuddha, a word which cannot be accurately defined, but which evidently implies an innate consciousness of truth.[1] Then he goes on to say: "I have no name, I seek no profit; but, to declare the truth, to save all living things from pain, to fulfil my ancient vow, to rescue all not yet delivered. I go to sound the law-drum (*i.e.*, to teach) in Benares." The young Brahman, astonished at the manner and the words of the Bhikshu, left him to pursue his journey: but yet he could not forget what he had heard. "At every turning of the road he stopped to think, embarrassed every step he took." The Buddha (called now Tathâgata, the "properly come"), proceeding slowly onwards, came to the Kasi city; there he seeks out the five hermits, who at first resolve to avoid and ignore him, but, as he approached, they rose and conducted him to a place of rest. And now Buddha is represented as turning the law-wheel of his doctrine, that is, laying the foundation of his authority as a teacher or preacher. He declares to the five men the character of his doctrine, embodied in four leading truths. First of all, he says, his is a middle way; he discountenances

[1] It seems to be allied to *συνείδησις*.

asceticism. "The emaciated devotee," he says, "produces in himself, by needless suffering, sickly and confused thoughts; for he who tries to feed a lamp with water will not succeed in scattering darkness, and so the man who tries with worn-out body to trim the lamp of wisdom, will not succeed, nor yet destroy his ignorance and folly." And then he goes on:—"Who seeks with rotten wood to evoke the fire [*i.e.*, by drilling one piece of wood into another] will waste his labour and get nothing for it; but drilling hard wood into hard the man of skill forthwith gets fire. So, in seeking wisdom, 'tis not by these austerities a man may reach the law of life." But, on the other hand, he continues, the way is not by pleasure or unrestraint, for "to indulge in pleasure is opposed to right,—this is the fool's barrier against enlightenment. As some man, grievously afflicted, eats food not fit to eat and aggravates his sickness, so how can he get rid of lust who pampers lust? Scatter the fire amid the desert grass dried by the sun, who shall put out the flames fanned by the wind? Such is the fire of 'hankering lust' [concupiscence]. I then," he adds, "reject both these extremes; my heart keeps in the middle way; all sorrow at an end and finished, now I rest in peace." Buddha then goes on to explain the eightfold path by which the same end is to be sought. Of this we shall speak hereafter. But this eightfold path is "the way," and "the way" is the last of the four truths. The three other truths are these:—Sorrow exists, and then he explains what sorrow is. And he sums up his definition in these words:—"The source of sorrow is in 'self' [I]; get rid of self, and sorrow ends." The second truth is, that sorrows accumulate, that is, that from this germ of self, countless sorrows grow and increase, amongst which old age and death are chief. The third truth is, these sorrows may be remedied. There is no hard and invincible fate or necessity in the case; but as sorrow began so it may end. And then the last truth before named comes in, "the way,"—the eightfold line of duty, by which the fetters one by one are loosed, and the condition of an Arhat—a saint—is obtained. This was Buddha's first sermon on the highest truth; "and having spoken thus respecting truth, the men and 80,000 of the *devas* were thoroughly embued with saving knowledge. They put away defilement from themselves; they got the eyes of the 'pure law' [*i.e.*, sight to behold the true teaching]; then all the earth-spirits together raised a shout triumphant, 'Well done! Tathâgata on this auspicious day has set revolving that which never yet revolved, and far and wide for gods and men has opened wide the gate *amatam*.'" I prefer leaving this last word untranslated, for it would be misleading to render it by our word "immortality," and yet it means deathlessness, or, according to Buddhaghosha, the great southern authority, it signifies that condition which, "not being born, does not decay nor die" ("Pāli Dict.," Childers, *sub voce*). This is the literal account given us by Asvaghosha of the first sermon preached by Buddha. We cannot here notice any other point respecting it than this, that the *devas*, or beings who correspond somewhat with our idea of angels, are made, in the

Buddhist dogma, hearers and learners of the doctrine as well as men. And countless numbers of these are represented as having been converted by the power of Buddha's teaching. In fact, the whole creation is brought within the same power, and from the lowest to the highest, for "all living," the teaching of the great sage is made serviceable.

We have, after this, an account of various incidents in the active life of Buddha as a teacher. To these it is unnecessary here to allude. He gathers round him disciples; travels from place to place; frames rules for his society or order; and brings the poor as well as the rich within the community. He allows women also, after some delay, to enter the order, and thus, during fifty years of life, he matures his system, and leaves behind for the guidance of his followers a body of well-digested rules. And now he comes to die: he is an old man of eighty, and he knows the end is near. The account of his last journey from Rājagriha to Kusinagara, as it is embodied in the "Mahâparinirvāna Sûtra," is precise, and probably authentic. It is found also in the concluding book of Asvaghosha's biography. There are one or two points in the narrative which deserve notice, and to these we will briefly allude. First, it is to be observed how the legend makes "the lord of the world of pleasure," *i.e.* Māra, constantly track the steps of the teacher. He had tried, in the first place, to prevent him from attaining a condition of enlightenment; afterwards he is described as coming to him on Mount Girsha to exhort him to leave the world; and now, on his journey towards the scene of his death, Māra again appears. The narrative, as it is found in Asvaghosha, runs thus :—Buddha had received the gift of a grove of trees from a woman (a courtesan), and was now about to leave Vaisâli—he was sitting down beside a pool or tank of water (the Markatahrada[1])—when, shedding forth a flood of glory from his person, Māra, the wicked one, was roused, and came to the place where Buddha was, and then, approaching with his hands closed, spake thus : "Formerly, beside the Nairanjanâ river, when you had accomplished your enlightenment, you said, 'When I have done all I have to do, then will I leave the world [pass to Nirvāna].' Now you have done all you had to do, you should, as then you said, depart." Then answered Buddha, "The time of my complete deliverance is near, but let three months elapse and I shall die." Then Māra joyously returned to heaven. Then Buddha declared, "Now have I given up my term of years. I live henceforth by power of spiritual ecstacy; my body like a broken chariot stands; completely freed from life [the world], I go enfranchised as a chicken from its egg."

Thus determined, the teacher is represented as travelling on slowly, accompanied by Ânanda, his personal attendant, "who loved so much," and his other disciples, towards Kusinagara. As he went, he preached his final sermons to the people of the various towns he passed. At length, arrived at Kusinagara, he took his seat between two sâla trees, and directed Ânanda to prepare his couch. "Ânanda going, and

[1] Asvaghosha, p. 267.

weeping as he went," obeyed the order. Then the Tathâgata lay down, his head towards the north, and on his right side, his hand beneath his head, with his feet crossed as any lion king. All grief is passed; from this one sleep his last-born body shall not rise again. His followers gather round him; the wind is hushed; the forest streams are silent; no sound is heard of bird or beast; the trees sweat out large flowing drops; the flowers and leaves fall mournfully: and thus he passed away; and then, as Buddha died, "the great earth quaked throughout; the sun and moon withdrew their shining; the sturdy forests shook like aspen leaves; whilst flowers and leaves untimely fell around like scattered rain."

CHAPTER IX.

SUBSEQUENT HISTORY OF BUDDHISM IN CHINA (HISTORICAL CONNEXION).

§ 1. It has been stated that a "Life of Buddha," similar to that of Asvaghosha's great poem, was brought to China so early as the year 70 A.D. From this date, for 600 or 700 years following, a succession of Buddhist monks or priests continued to arrive in that country. They brought with them their books, which, by the orders of various sovereigns, were translated and placed in the monasteries; and so, as these books accumulated, they were entered in the different catalogues prepared from time to time, and at length, in the year 684 A.D., grouped together as a collection or a body of sacred writings. It would be impossible even to allude to the work of each of the translators during this period, but some remarks may be made by way of illustration. In the first place, with respect to the motive that induced these priests to wander away from their native country across the mountains and deserts to China, doubtless the knowledge of so promising a field for work and the patronage given them would cause many to find their way eastwards. But there was also a strange impulse at work in the case of some of them "to convert the world," and it was this which constrained them to travel from spot to spot. Thus we read of a translator in the second century 147 A.D. who worked for forty years at Loyang in translating books, "moved by a desire to convert men."[1] Then immediately following him came a prince (so called, at least) of Parthia, who translated 176 distinct books. We should gladly know from what language these books were rendered, especially as we find one of them is the work called "Dharmapada," of which we shall speak further on, showing that this book was known even at this early time in the north. The expression generally used is, that these books were translated from the "Fan" language; but that is no guide, for the word does not necessarily mean the language of the Brahmans or of Brahmadeva, but it is used as a general term for all languages of India and the neighbouring countries. We are told[2] that, "at the time when the Tibetan books were translated, there existed Buddhist works in the language of Li [Khoten or Nepal], Zahora [the Panjāb], Kashmir, &c."; and there is no doubt such books were brought to China, for the translations frequently contain bastard proper names, and are evidently made from non-Sanscrit originals. But how soon books written in other than Indian dialects, commonly understood, for example, among the Parthians (the Arsacidæ), were brought to China is not determined. This much we know, that the last-named translator, who is called a prince, and who is said to have given up the kingdom to his uncle in

[1] Abstract of Four Lectures, p. 6.
[2] "Udánavarga," p. x.

order that he himself might become a Buddhist mendicant, was an Arsacid, and that he came to China A.D. 149 with books. Considering the important place Parthia held in the east at this time, and its close relation with the west, this point is an interesting one, but it is one we need not delay to consider further. It is plain, however, that many of the books translated were done from originals, not Sanscrit, but probably a corrupt dialect of Sanscrit commonly used in districts outlying the Indian frontier.

§ 2. It is noticeable how rapidly the Buddhist movement and a knowledge of the books spread through China. In 335 A.D. the Chinese were allowed to take monastic vows themselves, and as many as forty-two convents (or pagodas) had been built in Loyang alone. It appears that much of this popularity was the result of a pretended power to work miracles. We read of a priest called Buddhasiṇha who claimed this power about the date just named, and, in consequence of his imposture, he persuaded the prince of the Chau kingdom to permit his subjects to become monks. These miraculous powers were sometimes an assumed ability to mount into the air without assistance, to

> Hang, like Mahomet, in the air,
> Or St. Ignatius at his prayer;[1]

but generally these miracles were connected with the *S*arîras, or relics of Buddha, or some great Bodhisattva (saint); these were either some hair which would

[1] "Hudibras," "Gesta Roman.," i., 326.

stretch indefinitely, or a bone-relic that no power of man could break. But in no case were miraculous powers of a benevolent kind claimed; the signs, in fact, of their superior claims were wonder-working powers rather than miracles. In agreement with this, we find priests occasionally put to death for practising magical arts; the account given is "that they used wild music to win followers, taught them to dissolve all ties of kindred, and aimed only at murder and disturbance." No doubt, in India power to work wonders was widely claimed by the Buddhists, and the miraculous virtues of the *S*arîras of Buddha when deposited in *stûpas* is constantly referred to by the Chinese Buddhist pilgrims. Fă-hien, for example, tells us that when Buddha visited North India he left an impression of his foot in a kingdom called Udyâna, and that in his time the impression was still there; but, he adds, "it appears large or small according to the intensity of the religious feeling of the person who beholds it."[1] Again (p. 38, *op. cit.*), he tells us of Buddha's alms-bowl, "which poor people with a few flowers are able to fill, whilst the rich, though they offer thousands of bushels, can never fill." And every chapter in Hiouen Thsang's history of India contains accounts of wonders beyond all human ken wrought by the relics of Buddha. Sometimes the *stûpa* emits a constant flood of light; sometimes it has the power of effecting an answer to the prayers of worshippers; at other times, a cover remains in mid air suspended by nothing; at other times the

[1] Fă-hien, Beal's trans., p. 27.

cover moves with the worshipper. We cannot wonder, therefore, that these magical powers were referred to similar relics and buildings in China, and hence to a great extent the rapid growth in popularity of the new creed amongst the people. At the beginning of the Tang dynasty (620–904 A.D.), a persecution was raised against Buddhism on the ground that the priests and nuns, by avoiding marriage, impoverished the revenue—"what they hold about the condition of men depending on the will of Buddha is false; life and death are all determined by a self-governing fate; the monks are idle and unprofitable members of the community." So said Fu-yi, one of the ministers of Kaou-Tsu, the first emperor of this dynasty. After some controversy, the Confucianists gained their point, and severe restrictions were placed on the foreign faith. These, however, were shortly afterwards removed; and during the reign of the second emperor fresh honours were bestowed on the priests, and in the person of Hiouen Thsang, the pilgrim, the cause was made an occasion for high court favour. Yet we read in the annals of frequently-recurring persecutions. Early in the eighth century, A.D. 714, more than 12,000 priests were obliged to resume a secular life, and the writing of books, casting images, and building temples were strictly prohibited. But the cloud passed over, and in the year A.D. 763 Tae-tsung patronised the monks, because "he believed that by propitiating the unseen powers he could preserve his empire from danger at less cost than by expending blood and treasure on the battle-field." This at least was a business-like way of looking at the question. Again, the Emperor Hien-tsung sent mandarins to escort a bone of Buddha to the capital, on which one of his ministers presented a strongly-worded remonstrance to his master:—"Why should a decayed bone, the filthy remains of a man long dead, be introduced into the imperial residence? As for Buddha, he braved his vengeance and defied his power." This protest is still regarded with admiration by the Confucianists; the author of it, however, was banished to the Kwang-chow province, where some accounts state he was converted to Buddhism by a priest called Tai-Tien.

In the year 845 A.D., a third and very severe persecution broke out against the Buddhists. By an edict of the Emperor Wu-tsung, 4,600 monasteries were destroyed, and 40,000 smaller religious houses; the property of the houses was confiscated and used in the erection of secular buildings, and the copper bells and images were melted down and made into copper coins. More than 260,000 monks and nuns were made to return to secular life. Yet once again, as so frequently happens in history, this policy was reversed by Wu-tsung's successor, and unlimited tolerance proclaimed. Thus it was; the opposition of the Confucianists at one time was sufficient to check for awhile the advance of this creed—at another time, it recovered its lost numbers and seemed to ride over all misfortunes. At length we read of a census being taken, towards the end of the thirteenth century, of the number of Buddhist temples and monks in the country—of the former it was reported there were 42,318, and of the latter 213,148,—this was during the reign of Kublai Khan. If we remember that the ordained monks represent only a fractional portion of the professed adherents of the religion, and that beyond these again are the "unattached" professors or believers in the externals of religion, we may conclude that at this time a majority of the people of the empire were Buddhistic if not Buddhists.

So the religion fared, until the time of Kang-hi, the fourth emperor of the present Manchu dynasty (1662 A.D.), issued the so-called Sacred Edict, in which the Buddhists are blamed for fabricating groundless tales about future happiness and misery. They are charged with "doing this only for gain, and encouraging for the same object large gatherings of the country population at the temples, ostensibly to burn incense, but really to promote mischief." These sentiments are approved of at the present time. One of the sixteen lectures comprised in the edict is read at the periods of the new and full moon, in the temple of the patron god of each Chinese city. The town clerk, the local officers of Government, and a few rustic people, compose the audience. The Buddhist priests are denounced as drones of society, creatures like moths and mischievous insects, that thrive on the industry of others, whilst they do no work themselves. The people are warned not to go to their temples, nor take part in their village festivals. Thus ostensibly the religion is proscribed, but yet it flourishes. The temples are still frequented; the monasteries, especially about Pekin, are crowded with thousands and tens of thousands of monks, and books are issued from every quarter of the land, advocating or exhorting to the use of "the Scriptures." It is our duty to look below the surface of this matter, and inquire what it is in Buddhism that keeps its hold on the minds of the people of China and Japan; and whether we may not deal with the question in a manner more suited to our own advantageous position, and the wants of the people, than we seem to have done hitherto.

CHAPTER X.

BUDDHISM IN ITS PHILOSOPHICAL AND RELIGIOUS ASPECTS.

THE question whether we are to regard Buddhism merely as a philosophy has been frequently raised. "It must be kept in mind," says the Right Rev. Bishop Claughton, Archdeacon of London, "that Buddhism is rather a system of philosophy than a creed; and whilst it has a priesthood remarkable for their learning and the strictness of their rules of living, it does not profess to set before its followers an object of worship, or encourage them to place reliance on such acts of religious observance, as it permits rather than requires of them."[1] And this appears to be true, so far as the abstract principles of the system are concerned. But, practically, Buddhism is a religious system. It appeals to a principle of faith, it exacts worship, and it looks for reward hereafter. In China, at any rate, these points admit of no dispute; but it will be well to consider them for a while in detail.

1. Buddhism appeals to a principle of faith. The common remark made by the Chinese Buddhist pilgrim Hiouen Thsang, during his journeys through India, is that the people were either believers or

[1] Paper read before the Victoria Institute, January 19, 1874.

heretics. The former were Buddhists. What their belief amounted to, in some cases, we can hardly define: but this is the usual expression. We shall come to speak presently of the later objects which were introduced into the system, and which are specially named as demanding faith, such as Kwan-yin and Amitābha: for the present we confine ourselves to the earlier belief. The pilgrim just named particularises the three gems (*san paou*) as the objects of the faith of those who professed Buddhism. These three gems (*triratna* or *Ratnatraya:* the same as *san paou*) are explained as the treasure of Buddha, the treasure of the law, the treasure of the priesthood. It is in these the Buddhists, from the earliest days, "put their trust." This, evidently, amounts to faith in an object. It is true, these three objects may be, when analysed, nothing but "logical abstractions,"—undoubtedly, as idols, they are "nothing,"—but that does not alter the fact that they are believed in, and that, in consequence, the Buddhists have an object of faith. These objects are formally recognised by the convert as able to bring deliverance. Hence, the phrase used in Southern Buddhism, "I put my trust in Buddha, dharmas, saṇgha" (Buddhaṃ saraṇaṃ gacchámi, &c.), is rendered into Chinese by "I take my refuge in Buddha," &c. This denotes trust and reliance, and is an exercise of faith. How the convert can put his trust in that which, on his own ground, has passed away and does not exist is a point to be considered in its place, we here only state the case as brought before us in this *confessio fidei.*

2. But, secondly, this principle or confession of faith

exacts worship, or leads to worship. As to this, again, regarded on abstract principles, we agree with the authority before named: "Buddhism can have no worship, strictly speaking, to offer to its adherents as the expression of belief."[1] This is true, but in dealing with Buddhism we have to do with a fact, not a logical probability or possibility; we are brought into contact with people who undoubtedly *do* worship, and it is important to satisfy ourselves on the point, *What* do they worship? Perhaps the most interesting source of information on this point is the record found in the Buddhist sculptures. It is only within the last few years that this source of information has been before us. I will notice, first of all, the remains found at the great *tope* of Sanchi. Here we find proofs of the fact, that Buddhists worshipped so early, at least, as the date of these erections. Referring to the plates in Dr. Ferguson's "Tree and Serpent Worship," we find repeated scenes of such worship. Nor can we say that the tree is worshipped or the serpent either, for this were to misunderstand the whole subject. The "wheel"[2] is equally reverenced, and "umbrella,"[3] and in one case there is no object except Buddha himself to whom the reverence is offered.[4] It is, in fact, now settled, that these sculptures, as well as those at Amravati and at Bharhut, represent the character of Buddhist worship paid to the invisible presence of the Teacher, or to the power

[1] *Op. cit.*, p. 5.
[2] Plate xxix., figure 2.
[3] Plate xxxv., figure 2.
[4] Plate xxxi., figure 2.

supposed to reside in his teaching (the wheel). It is a worship of association or of memory. The spots rendered famous by Buddha's presence during his lifetime are consecrated in the mind of his disciple to the sacred recollection, and worship is offered on those spots to the invisible presence of the object of faith. And so, throughout India, the pilgrims tell us of countless sacred localities where Buddha or one of his predecessors had walked or taught, and on these spots sacred buildings were raised and worship paid. The story goes, in fact, that there were so early as the days of Asoka (*circ.* 230 B.C.) as many as 84,000 such spots. This may be, and probably is, an exaggeration, but that there were very many we cannot doubt, not only because they are named by the pilgrims, but because the remains still exist. We can have little doubt, then, that from early days, worship was offered by Buddhists at sacred spots, consecrated by the presence of the Teacher, to an invisible presence. This presence was formulated by the later Buddhists under the phrase "the body of the Law," *dharmakāya.* It was a necessity that led to the invention and employment of such a word, for we cannot doubt the Buddhists felt the inconsistency of apparently worshipping some thing that on their own confession had gone away and had no longer a personal existence. But Buddha, in his last discourse with his disciples, had told them: "After my Nirvāna ye ought to reverence and obey the law; receive it as your master, or as a light shining in the darkness, or as a precious jewel—the law that I have given, this you ought to obey and follow carefully, regarding it in no way different from myself." Here was the germ from which proceeded the idea or formula of an invisible presence; the teaching and power of the law (*dharma*) represented the *dharmakāya*, or law-body of Buddha, present with the order, and a fit object for reverence. In a curious inscription, written in Chinese character, and lately discovered in India, we have mention made of this body of the law. It appears that a religious disciple, called Ho-yun, had travelled from China to India (Gayâ, south of Patna) to "worship the sacred spots." Coming to Buddha Gayâ, the most sacred spot in the eyes of the Buddhist, he carved an inscription, and left it there (he lived A.D. 1022). In this we read of the three "bodies" of Buddha: first, his human body (Nirmānakāya); second, his Sâmbhoga body, or body of compensation, that is, the body assumed in the various forms under which Buddha appeared in his existences previous to his last birth; third, the dharmakāya, which is thus described in the inscription, "co-extensive with the universe, inhabiting all time, with excellences innumerable as the dust-grains, beyond all human character, transcending all human language." Such was the conception of the invisible body worshipped by the devotees who visited the sacred spots, and also by the human and divine or superhuman beings represented in the early sculptures prostrate in adoration before the seat or throne, and tantamount to an altar, where Buddha had sat and was now adored. This point appears to be an important one to settle, for it leads us to consider how nearly it is possible for the human mind to approach the secret made known to us with regard to the spiritual character of the Supreme God. There is scarcely need to say that this form of worship is still used among the Buddhists. It has greatly changed, and amounts now to an idolatry, the worship of an outward symbol, sometimes a gross and debasing idolatry; but yet, as a Buddhist priest in China told a missionary, the use of images is allowed for the ignorant or the weak, it is quite possible to worship without an image or any visible representation.[1]

We cannot pass by the worship of relics so commonly observed in the Buddhist community. This form of superstition, for it cannot be called idolatry as the object is not in most cases visible, began from the commencement of the Buddhist system. Whether it had been practised in India before the death of the last Buddha is not well determined. According to Buddha's directions, he was to be buried as a Chakravarttin or universal sovereign. This burial of wheel-kings or paramount sovereigns seems to allude to the Scythian custom of raising mounds over the remains of their leaders and paying them reverence. "We Scythians [Sâkas] have neither towns nor cultivated lands," they said to Darius, "if, however, you must come to blows with us speedily, look you now, there are our fathers' tombs, seek them out, and attempt to meddle with them, then ye shall see whether or no we will fight with you."[2] This was the sacredness attached to Buddha's burial-place. We may briefly quote the record as found in A*s*vaghosha; he has just

[1] "Catena of Buddhist Scriptures," p. 249.

[2] Herod., iv., 127; "Catena of Buddhist Scriptures," p. 127.

died between the sâla trees at Kusinagara :—" Then on a gold and silver gem-decked couch, richly adorned with flowers and scents, they [*i.e.* the people of the city, the Mallas, in conjunction with the disciples] placed the body of Tathâgata ; a jewelled canopy they raised above, and round it flags and streamers and embroidered banners ; then, using every kind of dance and music, the lords and ladies of the Mallas followed along the road presenting offerings ; whilst *devas* scattered scents and flowers and raised the sounds of music in the sky. Entering the city, there the men and women, old and young, joined in the worship. Crossing the river then, they placed above the body sandal wood and every famous scented wood, and poured upon the whole unguents and oil of every sort. Then placing fire beneath, three times they walked around. . . . The scented oil consumed, the fire declines, the bones they place within a golden pitcher [vase], to remain until the world shall pass away. They placed the relics then upon a tower for men and *devas* to adore." The account then goes on to explain how these relics were divided into eight portions, and given to eight representative people, and over them *stûpas*, mounds faced with stones, erected. It is to these *stûpas*, containing the relics, worship is paid, or, rather, before these *stûpas* or *chaityas* worship is paid to the relics enshrined within. There is a typical example of this kind of worship in "Tree and Serpent Worship," pl. xxviii., fig. 1. Here we see a northern race of people, Scyths, paying reverence to the relics in the *stûpa* before them. There is reason to believe that this scene relates to the *chaitya* or *stûpa* erected by the people of Vaisâlî who were probably a northern race. The question arises: Did these people introduce this form of worship into India? If we might think so, it would simplify matters very much, for we should be able to connect the worship of the northern races paid to their fathers' tombs with this relic worship in India through the intervention of the northern race who occupied the neighbourhood of Vaisâlî. But, in any case, the worship existed from an early time. It is curious to note how, in later days, the *chaitya* or relic-shrine occupied the extreme east part of the cave temples or Indian basilicas. It is always found in the chord of the apse, and so placed that the worshippers may perform around it the customary perambulation (*pradakshina*) from left to right, *i.e.*, keeping the right shoulder or hand always to the object to be adored, even as in the first record already quoted we read, "three times they walked around." From this early custom proceeded the now universal habit of worshipping relics preserved among Buddhists everywhere. The great Burmese Tope Shuay Dagon is supposed to enshrine some hair and nail parings of the Teacher. The *delada*, or tooth relic, at Ceylon, and the worship paid to it, is well known, and throughout India, in the days of Hiouen Thsang and his predecessors, these relic-shrines abounded, and their fame was so well established as to bring thousands of worshippers to the spot. In China, also, there have been found relics, and shrines have likewise been erected over them, which are objects of worship. The following is an account of one, extracted from the journal of some missionaries who journeyed into the interior of China some twenty-five years ago[1]: "In the evening we went to the temple of Asokarâśa, where there was said to be a Sarîra (*shay-li*), or relic of Buddha. The priests were at vespers when we went in, but on our expressing a desire to see the relic one of them agreed to show it to us. On going to the bell-shaped dome in which it is placed, he could not unlock the little door, whereupon he called to one of his brother-priests, who was then kneeling down at his prayers, to come and help him. This the latter did, chanting his prayers as he came along; between them the door was opened and the relic brought out. It was said to be contained in a little carved box of a pyramidal shape,[2] and we were told to look into it against the light, which was then fast declining, to discern the wonder. But whether it was owing to the shades of evening having set in, or to the light of Buddha not having yet dawned upon us, we could see nothing. We asked the priests where the relic was obtained, they replied, at the top of the neighbouring hill. We then asked how they knew it was a relic of Buddha. They said they had no proof, but their forefathers had handed it down as a relic of Buddha, and as such they received it. They said that sometimes it shone out with great brilliancy, but to those who had no faith it did not condescend to

[1] "Shanghai Almanack," 1857.

[2] Compare the remark of Clemens Alexandrinus with respect to the Semnoi (Buddhists): *σέβουσί τινα πυράμιδα ἐφ' ἣν ὀστέα τίνος Θεοῦ νομίζουσιν ἀποκεῖσθαι.*—Strom. III. vii.

shine at all. In that case, we said, we shall most likely continue in ignorance, as we have no faith in Buddha; this did not seem to affect the priests, nor did they seem to care much for the honour of the system by which they got their bread." This will illustrate our point.

There is, however, no worship of a Supreme Being known among Buddhists, and here is the radical defect of the system. They worship, but the purpose of their worship is to express a feeling of reverence for that which ought to be revered, a principle rather than an object. But yet, so strong is the impulse in the mind to worship something, they attach to these outward memorials, trees, *stûpas*, and even images, the memory of their Teacher, and worship them. Here is an interesting story told in one of Asvaghosha's sermons which will illustrate this point. It is related of a man who stole a jewel from a Buddhist monument, and was brought to repentance by the leniency of the king: "I heard long ago this story about the lion-country [Ceylon]. There was once a man who procured a gem [Maṇi, a topaz], as large as his fist. This gem he presented to the king. The king, beholding it, said:—

> From days of yore, successive kings,
> Collecting gems, have sought renown;
> And when the tribute-bearers came,
> Have showed their jewels to exalt themselves;
> But, when these monarchs came to die,
> Their treasures all were left behind.

And so he resolved to get for himself the merit of charity which would follow him into the other world.

Accordingly he went to a neighbouring *stûpa*, and placed the jewel on the top of the spire that surmounted it. The light was like that of a bright star, so that the king's palace was lit up with its brightness. One day the light disappeared, and, on sending to find out the reason, the officers of the king found the pole lying at the foot of the *stûpa* and the jewel gone. Tracing some blood-tracks, they found the thief concealed in a neighbouring wood, with the jewel on his person. Seizing the man, they brought him to the king, who was at first indignant with the thief, but afterwards relented. The ministers advised his instant death, but the king replied: 'If he were put to death, what more could we do? But if his life be spared, we may perhaps raise him up from his great fall'; and then he added these verses:—

> We ought to try to rescue
> One so grievously fallen!
> I will give him gold and gems,
> Let him repent and get some merit,
> Perhaps he may escape
> From falling into misery!
> I will give him money;
> Let him offer gifts to Buddha!
> A man who falls by accident
> May, perchance, be raised again.

Then the king, giving the man money, bade him offer it to Buddha and wipe out his guilt. Then the thief, moved by the king's exercise of mercy, thought how wonderful a thing the religion of Buddha was to make the king so tender and forgiving. Having thought thus, he went straightway to the *stûpa*, and falling on his knees, he adored and said: 'Great merciful! Lord of the world! Although thou hast passed into Nirvāna, yet thy favour can find out me!

> The world names you true saviour,
> Let this deliverance find me out!
> Now in my affliction
> Let thine image bring me rest.' "

This is the purport of the story—it illustrates the adoration paid by Buddhists to objects associated with the memory of Buddha's presence. The worship is more a subjective yearning of the heart, moved by a feeling of want, than the homage of worship paid to a living and personal deity. But still, in its outward aspect, and in one sense viewed from within, it is the worship of creatures ignorant of their Creator.

The same remarks will apply to the utterance of prayers or vows, or earnest desires, in the presence of such objects as these. It is plain, there can be no prayer addressed to a living god; but yet the Buddhists pray in the sense of uttering their "soul's desire." It is a yearning for help, a subjective struggle by which the end is obtained *ex opere operato*. There is the same evidence in this case as in the last: the records of Hiouen Thsang and Fa-hien relate many incidents in which the use of prayer is implied. For example, when Fa-hien was returning from Ceylon to China by sea, a storm rose, and the ship was in imminent danger. The pilgrim was only afraid lest the merchants should wish to throw overboard his sacred books and images to lighten the ship, and so with earnest heart he invoked (prayed to) Avalokitesvara, and called upon all the Buddhist saints of China, speaking thus: "I have wandered far in quest of religious books. Oh! by your spiritual power bring me back and let me reach my resting-place! Nevertheless," he continues, "the hurricane blew for thirteen days and nights." This worship of Avalokitesvara we shall consider hereafter. He is assumed to be a living god; but not so with Buddha,—the prayers offered to him are offered as an exercise of inward emotion, and in expectation of a self-working cure; like the snake that struggles from its skin, they are in the Buddhist's view the struggle of the heart to free itself from that which holds and binds it to the illusions of the world.

3. But this subject will be illustrated further by considering, thirdly, that the Buddhist is affected by hope of the future in the exercise of his religious instincts. It is this hope or longing for something better that makes him worship and appear to pray. It is first of all a hope of final deliverance—deliverance from sorrow. Sorrow, we remember, is the great evil, according to Buddhist teaching—the great evil ruling the world. To escape from sorrow is the aim, and to be able to effect this in the use of the means, or in the "right way," is the hope of the disciple. We shall not attempt to define Nirvāna, at least for the present; it is sufficient to state, and this admits of no contradiction, that this condition, whatever it be, is the hope of the Buddhist. If it be extinction of being, still this, including in it rescue from trouble, is desired. If it be a positive condition of rest, this also, implying deliverance, is his hope. It

is plain, however, that this hope is not an immediate one. He may have to wander through countless births ere he attain it, yet it is not lost sight of. But his immediate hope is a birth in heaven, or, to put it more generally, happiness in the other world; hence we meet with such declarations as the following: "The rewards of the righteous and the unrighteous are not the same; the unrighteous go to hell, the righteous find their way to happiness [heaven]."

"Perform carefully the precepts of the law [religion], abstain from all evil deeds; he who keeps the law finds happiness in this world and the next." "He who, seeking happiness, persecutes and punishes other beings also seeking for happiness, will not find happiness in the other world."

Such sentences might be produced in great numbers; but it may be assumed as a fundamental truth that the Buddhist hopes for, and seeks after, happiness in the other world. And yet it is not his final hope, such a sentence as the following will show us that: "Worldly happiness and happiness in the region of the gods is not worth the sixteenth part of the happiness resulting from the destruction of desires." In fact, to desire to be born in heaven as the "end" is contrary to the plain teaching of the system: for the gods are subject to death. They also must return to other forms of life, perhaps with men, perhaps in the "evil ways," and therefore to desire birth in heaven as a complete reward is forbidden by Buddha. Hence Asvaghosha lays down this principle, although a man keep the precepts, if he does so with a view to obtain a heavenly reward (or the pleasures of heaven), he does but break the precepts. And to exemplify this, he adds a story of which the following is the substance: A Shaman, *i.e.*, a disciple of Buddha, observing a Brahman undergoing painful penance, asked him what he expected to result from his self-imposed austerities. He replied that he hoped hereafter to be born as a king, on which the Shaman expostulates with him, and asks what pleasure can there be in such a hope—"What happiness in such a state? 'Tis like a fish that nibbles at the bait, or like the honey covering up the knife, or like the net or baited trap, the fishes or the beasts desire to taste, but see not their impending suffering. The case is so with worldly happiness; we now enjoy our luxuries, but in the end are born in hell. Consider then and weigh the matter; the joys to be partaken of, how few! the pain and suffering, how great! Ponder well and recollect the pain, and seek not happiness like this. Let go your grasping, covetous mind, and seek to find entire escape."

And so throughout this and other works, as an essential principle, we find the hope of heaven as a sufficient reward discountenanced, the only complete enjoyment is in the final rest of Nirvāna.

But yet again, as a way to this final escape, a birth in heaven is a strong desire with the faithful Buddhist. The account given us of Hiouen Thsang's death will illustrate this. He was, as we have before stated, one of the Chinese pilgrims who had left his country to visit India and collect books. He had now returned home with a great quantity of relics, images, and religious books; many of the last he had translated. He had just finished the translation of the "Mahâ prajñâ pâramitâ sûtra," which formed 600 books in 120 volumes. "During the time that the master was translating this work, he thought constantly on death. 'Now,' he said, one day, to his religious friends, 'now I am sixty-five years of age. The work on which I am engaged is extremely long, I fear every moment I shall die before it is finished. Redouble your efforts; let no fatigue interfere with your zeal in helping me to accomplish the task.' After finishing it, the master felt his powers of body and mind to be decreasing and knew his end was approaching. Addressing his disciples, he said: 'After my death, when you take me to my last home, let it be in a simple and modest way. Wrap my body in a mat, and place it in some quiet and secluded valley. Let it not be placed in the neighbourhood of a royal palace or a convent; for a body impure as mine should not lie in such a place.' His disciples hearing his words gave way to cries and tears; but at length, on the twenty-third day, the end approached. He gave away alms in charity for the poor, and then called all the members of the convent to his bedside, 'to bid adieu to his impure and despicable body.' 'I desire,' he said, 'to see the merit of my good deeds returned on all mankind; I desire to be born in the heaven called Tusita [the happy or joyous]; to be admitted among the disciples of Maitreya ["the loving," the future Buddha], and there to serve him as my tender and affectionate lord. I desire to be born in future births here on earth, that I may accomplish with unceasing zeal my duties to the Buddha, and at length arrive at the condition of perfect wisdom [the unsurpassed condition of wisdom (*bodhi*)].' After uttering his adieux, he lay in meditation; then, as he sank, regretting that he had made so little progress towards the fulness of intelligence, he pronounced two verses :—

'Adoration to Maitreya! gifted with sublime intelligence. I desire [pray] to be allowed with all men to behold your face.

'Adoration to Maitreya! I desire [pray] to be admitted after death to your presence and the multitude which dwells around you!'

Thus he lay without movement. In the middle of the night his disciples asked him: 'Master, have you yet obtained a birth in heaven [Maitreya's heaven]?' 'Yes,' he whispered, and with sinking voice he breathed his last."

Here we see the character of the mistaken hope of the Buddhist. He does not expect as yet complete deliverance (Nirvāna), but he desires to be born where Maitreya, who shall come as Buddha to the world, is now engaged with a great multitude, teaching and directing them. So the hope is strengthened that in time the end may be accomplished and the coveted Nirvāna reached.

So far, it would seem, Buddhism has a right to be called a religious system; it appeals to a principle of faith, or at any rate of trust; it has a form of worship and of prayer, even if it be allowed that the worship and prayer are offered up to an abstraction; and it admits of the exercise of hope in some future good; the good may be ill-understood, but it is in itself an end of sorrow and a state of rest. Ere that is reached, there may be countless births to be experienced, but in each the good work (merit) of the former lives weighs in the scale and brings complete deliverance ever nearer.

From what has been said, we see that there is a religious element in Buddhism, *i.e.*, Buddhism as it was first taught. This character is essential to the system as it developed and as it now exists in China. What this amounted to in India, at a later date, we have told us by one of the Chinese pilgrims. We have seen from Hiouen Thsang's frequent mention of worship paid before *stûpas*, and prayers offered up in sacred places, that the character of a religion was given it in his time. We find from another pilgrim who lived about the same time, viz., I-tsing, what this worship amounted to: "This pilgrim was born in T'si-chan, in the province of Shan-tung. His family name was Chang, his private name was Wen. He became a disciple when very young, and at fifteen years of age resolved to visit the western world. In the year 671 A.D., he set out by sea from Canton, and after visiting Java[1] and other places among the Southern Islands, he came to India. Having passed through more than thirty countries, he returned homewards. Arrived in China after twenty years' absence, he devoted himself to the work of translation. He brought back with him one picture of the diamond-throne [*i.e.*, the seat on which Buddha obtained enlightenment] and 300 fragments of relics [*śarîras*]; he, moreover, brought nearly 400 volumes of books, containing 500,000 verses."

[1] Śribhoja, probably the coast of Sumatra, near the Equator.

From one of the books he wrote, we find what the Buddhist service was like in his days in India. He says ("Nan-hae-kí-kwei-chŭn," § 32) :—"In India the *chaityas* which stand by the roadside are reverenced by all the passers-by. Every evening the monks come from the convents they occupy and walk three times round these *stûpas* [*i.e.*, those belonging to their respective establishments], they pass round them in procession, scattering flowers and burning incense; then, sitting down, some skilful brother with clear voice chants the praises of the great Master; for this purpose they have hymns, consisting of ten or even twenty verses. They then return to the Temple, and, having taken their seats in the preaching hall, a preacher mounts the pulpit and there reads a short sermon [*sûtra*]. The pulpit is not far from the president's [*sthavira*] throne; but it is not so high nor so large. Whilst reading the *sûtra*, they often chant a piece from the collection of hymns compiled by A*s*vaghosha; and they also frequently recite the hymn of praise to the three honoured names. After singing, they march in procession round the apse three times. They then say, 'saddhu' [it is well], and the preacher descends from his pulpit. The president then rises and bows to the lion throne,[1] afterwards to the assembled brethren, and then resumes his seat. The second priest then bows to the pulpit and the assembly, and then salutes the president and sits down. The third priest does likewise, and so throughout the assembly.

[1] That is, the pulpit.

If the number of priests is very great, then three or five, as they think proper, rise at the same time and salute as before. This done, they break up the congregation. This is the rule," he continues, "of the priesthood throughout the holy land of India, from Tamralipti [at the mouth of the Ganges] to the convent of Nâlanda [near Patna]. In the latter establishment the number of priests and disciples is so great, amounting to about 5,000, that such an assembly in one place would be difficult. The great temple, therefore, has eight halls, and in these the various congregations assemble. The rules of worship here are somewhat different from those ordinarily followed. They choose one singing master [precentor], who every evening goes through the different halls where the brethren are assembled, and accompanied by a pure-brother [a novice?], who precedes him with flowers and incense. As they pass through the assemblies, the members of the congregation bow down, and, as they are thus bowing, they repeat a hymn of three or five verses, accompanied by music. At sunset the officiating brother receives an offering [a certain allowance as an offering], and then singly chants before the censer [incense heap] a hymn of praise. Then the congregation give three complete prostrations, and the assembly is broken up. This is the traditional custom of worship in the west. The old and sick occupy seats apart from the rest." Such is the substance of I-tsing's account of Buddhist worship in India in the seventh century. We have no earlier account than this; but, from the construction of the *stûpas*, round which we find a procession path, and from the character of the *chaitya* caves, in which the *stûpa* is placed in the apse evidently for the purpose of processional investment, there can be little doubt that some such form of worship prevailed from early days. In China, the character of Buddhist worship offered (to Kwan-yin particularly) is well known, and is very singular. We will briefly allude to this.

CHAPTER XI.

THE WORSHIP OF KWAN-YIN.

THIS is the most common object of veneration among the Buddhists in China. Kwan-yin is a contraction of Kwan-shai-yin, a phrase signifying "a being who hears or perceives the cries of men." We will speak of this being, as is usual among the Chinese, as a female Pu-sa, or goddess. She is commonly known as the "Goddess of Mercy," from her attribute of "hearing." It is evident at once that such a being is foreign to the principles of Buddhism. There is no object of supreme worship among the Buddhists of the southern school. We must look on this culture, then, as a foreign introduction. The Indian name for Kwan-yin is Avalokite*s*vara, the "looking-down god," and the idea of such a being was probably derived from the old worship paid to the gods of the hills. It seems probable that this Avalokite*s*vara was at first identical with Sumana, the god supposed to reside on Adam's peak in Ceylon. Reasons for this supposition will be given hereafter; it is enough now to say that this mount was visited (according to the legend) by Buddha, who left here an impression of his foot; according to the words of the "Mahavamsa," chap. i., "rising aloft in the air, the divine teacher displayed the impression of his foot on the mountain of Sumanekuto," *i.e.*, Adam's peak. But, in the north, the legend is narrated under another form, viz., that Buddha visited Lanka, *i.e.*, Ceylon, and whilst there preached on Mount Potaraka or Potalaka a *sútra*, called Avalokitesvara, "with twelve faces."[1] Now, the name given to this being by M. Burnouf is *Samanta Mukha* ("Lotus of the Good Law," chap. xxiv.), or, "the god who looks every way"; and one name of Sumana, the genius of the mountain, is Samanta, and the peak is called Samanta kuta, so that we cannot doubt that Avalokitesvara (or the god who looks down, *i.e.*, from the height of the mountain top) "with twelve faces," is the same as Samanta.[2] This is rendered more likely if we consider the origin of the word Potaraka, or Potalaka. It is exactly the same word which is applied to Patala, at the mouth of the Indus, whence Nearchus with his fleet set out on their return homewards. Whatever the true origin of this word, it means undoubtedly a harbour or a place for boats. Arrian tells us that the Indians call all the deltas at the mouths of their rivers "Patalas"; but this was probably hearsay only, as there is no such Indian word.[3] General Cunningham supposes the origin of the word to be the Sanscrit Pâṭala, a trumpet-flower, because of its shape, "in allusion to the trumpet shape of the province included between the eastern and western branches of

[1] "Memorials of Sâkya Buddha," § 94.

[2] Childers, "Pāli Dictionary," *sub voc.*; also Spence Hardy, "Manual of Buddhism," p. 211.

[3] Arrian, "Exped. Alex.," *lib.* v., p. 200, ed. Gronovii.

the mouth of the Indus, as the two branches as they approach the sea curve outwards like the mouth of a trumpet";[1] but this seems far-fetched. It would appear more probable that Potala was an old word for "harbour," or "place for boats"; at least, we find the word *pota*, a boat, an old Sanscrit word, and the termination *la* (or *loka*) a frequent one to signify "that which holds or keeps"; the word Potala, "the name of a seaport on the Indus,"[2] with which the Potalaka mountain is connected,[3] would therefore signify the harbour or boat-place. But there was also a Patala in Ceylon, and it was the harbour usually frequented by foreign ships; it is the present Putlam, formerly called Bhatala, and by Ibn Battuta, Battāla. Concerning this port, Dr. Lee, in his "Hebrew Dictionary," has the following remarks[4]:—"If the Ophir from which this wood [the aloe] was brought was Ceylon, as Bochart seems to have shown ('Canaan,' *lib*. i. xlvi.), let us see whether we can find any such wood there. Ibn Battuta (p. 184, Lee's trans.) tells us that the whole shore of Battāla abounded with cinnamon-wood and the Kalangi aloe, and that the merchants of Malabar and of the Maabar districts transport it without any other price than a few articles of clothing, &c." This name of Putlam or Battāla, then, is connected with the mountain Potalaka. It was, doubtless, given to the mountain by those who visited the island and frequented this port—the mountain

[1] "Ancient Geography of India," p. 285.

[2] Monier Williams, "Sanskrit Dictionary," p. 598, c. 3.

[3] *Ibid.*

[4] Page 34, *sub voc.* אַלְמֻגִּים.

itself being visible to sailors nine days before reaching the land (Ibn Battuta). But this same name of Potaraka, under the form of P'u-to, is given to an island in the Chusan archipelago in China. These islands of Chusan lie just off the entrance to the great port of Hang-chau, from which in old time (and to the present day) the great trading junks (called Chinchew junks) set sail for their distant voyages. The name of Potalaka or P'u-to, therefore, was given to this island, and the goddess Kwan-yin, or Avalokite*s*vara, worshipped there; just as the Arab traders or others gave the name Potalaka to the mountain in Ceylon as the first land made on their adventurous voyages, and in both cases called Potala, from its proximity to the harbour, which they desired to find. So the god who looks down, viz., Sumana, or Avalokite*s*vara, was worshipped in both places. But there is a fourth Potaraka consecrated to the worship of this deity, viz., that in Tibet, where Llhasa is built. This, doubtless, is so consecrated in recollection of the origin of the *cultus*, viz., that of a hill-god who looks down; for this mountain of Potaraka in Tibet is one of the highest in that land of mountain ranges, and the god Kwan-yin, or Avalokite*s*vara, is the tutelary deity of the whole district. From what circumstance, then, did the worship of this being originate? It is highly probable that the merchants residing at Kandy, in the time of Fa-hien, and called by him Sa-pho, were Sabæans from the coast of Arabia.[1] The trade being in their hands, they had taken up their residence in

[1] Fah-hien (Beal's translation), p. 154.

the island, and would, doubtless, introduce many traditions from their own country into the place of their residence. Now, we are told by Tiele[1] that "in the religion of the Sabæans of South Arabia, made known to us by the decipherment of the Himyaritic inscriptions, by the side of the national gods of a genuinely Arabic character, such as the principal god Al-makah, 'the god who hearkens,' we meet with a number of purely Babylonian-Assyrian deities." This principal god, Al-makah, is found named in nearly all the Himyaritic records deciphered by M. Halévy and others.[2] It might be supposed, therefore, that these Sabæan merchants would bring some knowledge of such a famous god into Ceylon. We are not surprised, therefore, to find that the Chinese merchants, who went back from Ceylon and introduced the knowledge of Mount Potaraka, with its tutelary deity of Sumana, or Avalokitesvara (Samanta), carried back also the knowledge of this name, "he who hears," or, "the god who hearkens"; and this is the meaning of Kwan-yin, "the god who hears the cries of men" (Kwan-shai-yin). If this be so, here is a full explanation of the foreign character of this worship. As we said before, the idea of an objective worship is unknown to the early Buddhists. Whatever adoration was offered to the spots consecrated by Buddha's presence was offered as a subjective act, working as an *opus operatum*, and so also with regard to prayer; but now we see "an object" of worship introduced, and veritable worship and prayer offered to it. This

1 "Outlines of History," p. 79.
2 "Journal Asiatique," Octobre, 1873, vii. Série, tome ii.

cultus, then, is the result of a necessity felt by the worshippers, who could never rest satisfied with the adoration of a logical abstraction or an invisible presence. We will confirm this historical connexion by one or two further remarks. We are told by Dr. Edkins that "the worship of Kwan-yin was introduced into Indian Buddhism not long before the Christian era.[1] In China, Kwan-yin was worshipped probably as early as the Han dynasty [*i.e.*, down to 190 A.D.]." It was just at this time that the Arab sailors, by the discovery of the monsoons, traded regularly with South India and Ceylon. We might naturally expect to find this worship of Kwan-yin appearing in India at the same time.

But the worship of Kwan-yin is always associated with that of another deity called Amitābha, and their residence is in Sukhâvatî, or the land of the blest. But it is tolerably certain that the idea of Sukhâvatî is derived from the old name of Socotra, viz., Sukhadhara, the happy land. There is a remark made by the old geographer Agatharcides, in his work "De Mari Erythræo," § 102, that the happy islands lie off the mouth of the Red Sea, on which the editor of the "Geog. Græc. Minores" (Müller) has this note, "Certius est sermonem esse de mari extero, ubi Aden erat Sabæorum portus . . . . insulas beatas navigatorum ex Indiâ Arabiam petentium stationes, quasnam potissimum designare auctor voluerit, quæritur . . . . at ipsa beatarum insularum denominatio ad hodiernum ducit Socotora insulam, quam veteres geographi

[1] "Buddhism in China," p. 382.

Dioscoridæ insulam vocare solent, hoc enim nomen natum est ex Indico *dvipa sukhatara*, *i.e.*, insula beata sive fortunata, uti post Bochartum ('Geog. Sacr.' I. 1., p. 436) monuerunt Bohlen Ind. II. 139, Lassenius Benfey, Ritterus, alii." Now Agatharcides tells us that on this island merchants from all parts, especially near the Indus, congregated (§ 103) ; and the author of the "Periplus" says that the Sabæans were accustomed from this island to set out on their voyage to Ceylon, and it was here they collected their goods. We argue, therefore, that the knowledge of this Sukhadhara, or Sukhâvatî, island was brought to Ceylon by the same channel as the worship of the "hearing God," Al-makah, viz., by the Arab sailors who at an early date traded with the island, and many of whom settled in the chief town of Kandy, and were known to Fa-hien (A.D. 400). There is a remarkable confirmation of the supposition, that Socotora was from a very early period regarded as the island of the blessed, in some Egyptian records lately deciphered. In a paper read by Mr. W. Golenischeff at the Oriental Congress[1] in Berlin, "On an old Egyptian story," it is stated that in a papyrus he had just discovered in the "Hermitage Impérial" at St. Petersburg, he found an account of a voyage to the land of Poun-t, which it appears represents the two coasts of the Red Sea opposite each other at the straits of Bab-el-mandeb—the ship was 150 cubits long, 40 cubits broad, and manned by 150 of the best sailors of Egypt. A storm having arisen, the ship was

[1] "Transactions of the Oriental Congress," vi. p. 100.

lost whilst they were on the sea, as it seems, beyond the straits, and the narrator was the only one of the crew saved. He was carried, as he clung to a spar, to an island, where he passed three days in entire solitude. At length he went to search for something to eat, and he found figs and grapes, every sort of magnificent Aaqt, the fruits Kaou and Neqou, melons of all kinds, fishes, and birds—nothing was wanting. He dug a pit, lit a fire, and offered a sacrifice to the gods. Suddenly he heard a noise like the roaring of the sea, the trees shook, and the earth quaked again; and he found that the commotion was caused by a serpent that was approaching him; it was 30 cubits long, and its beard more than 2 cubits, its members (scales) were encrusted with gold and of the colour of the true lapis (lazuli). It coiled itself up in front of him. The narrator was filled with fear, and fell down before the creature. He goes on to tell how the serpent carried him in his mouth to a place of safety, and listened to his tale of shipwreck. "Fear not! fear not!" the creature said, "it is God who has preserved your life, and brought you to this enchanted isle. Nothing is wanting here; it is filled with everything that is good. You shall pass four months here, and then a ship will come with sailors and you shall return to your own town and die there." Accordingly, after the time stated, he descended to the shore, and there he found a ship manned with sailors who brought him back to the land of Pharaoh. This papyrus, Mr. Golenischeff tells us, is extremely ancient, reaching back nearly 4,000 years. He connects with this ancient story of the enchanted island the tale of the adventures of Ulysses, and the Arab story of Sinbad. We need not follow him here, but pass on to his statement respecting the island off the coast of Poun-t. He says, p. 112: "We have an inscription of the valley of Hammamât in which there is an account of a voyage of a certain Hannou, which he had undertaken in obedience to the orders of the Pharaoh Seanχkara, to the land of Poun-t, and which in style resembles the narrative found in the papyrus. In this account there is also mention made of a serpent, set to guard the incense accumulated on an island." Where then is this island? The translator of the story says: "the description of the island of paradise, as we find it in the papyrus, appears to explain itself naturally enough. The description of the island of Socotora leaves no doubt that the Egyptians who visited the land of Poun-t, very little distance from Socotora, were able, if not to see it, to hear accounts, more or less confused, which would give them an idea of that island, difficult of access, but rich in vegetation above all those on the north-east of Africa." If this conjecture be true, it would seem that the tale of "an island of paradise" must date from this old Egyptian belief, and the locality be identified with the isle of Socotora. In any case, this agrees remarkably with the Buddhist story of Sukhâvatî, or Sukhadhara, which is only another form of the word Socotora. It will, perhaps, be useful to give here the account of this supposed paradise, where Amitābha and Kwan-yin dwell.

CHAPTER XII.

THE WESTERN PARADISE OF THE BUDDHISTS.

THE worship of Amitābha under the corrupted form *O-me-to*, is a prevalent form of superstition in China. The word "Amitābha" means "boundless glory, or light." He is regarded as the father of Kwan-yin. In this connexion the worship was probably derived from Persia. He is the same as Mithras. He is also called Amitāyus, *i.e.*, "the Eternal." In this aspect he would correspond with the Persian "Zervan Akarana," or "boundless time." It was during the time of Artaxerxes Mnemon (*circ.* 380 B.C.) that the worship of Mithras, combined with foreign usages, spread over Western Asia to Europe, and in connexion with Anāhita (the goddess of pure water) was more widely diffused than that of any other deity of antiquity (Tiele). Hence among the altars found in such numbers on the Roman wall that stretches across our own island, not a few have been found dedicated to Mithras.

But we are told again by M. Reinaud (Ind. Ant., p. 335) that "the worship of the sun, and of the goddess Nanœa or Anaitis at an early date penetrated the whole of the Indus valley." This double worship probably gave rise to the Buddhist fiction of Amitābha and Kwan-yin. The latter, at any rate, has several of the attributes of the Persian Anāhita, Anaitis, or Nanœa. In the first place, she is worshipped as a female deity: she is also distinctly called "the pure" (*tsing*) as Anāhita was; again, she is called "the high" (*kao wang*) corresponding to Ardvi, the epithet of Anāhita (*Ardvi sura Anāhita*); she is drawn sitting beside "a waterfall" (Bunyiu Nanjio's Catalogue of the Chinese and Japanese books in the Bodleian, p. 7), thus indicating her association with "water"; and lastly, as Dr. Edkins tells us, the epithet of the Kwan-yin worshipped in P'uto is *Kwo-hai*, "she who came across the sea."

Without dilating on this point, it will be enough to state that the double worship of Amitābha and Kwan-yin holds a conspicuous place in the Buddhism of the North. It is associated with a fiction of a paradise, or, "happy, or, pure land." We cannot doubt the idea of such a land is derived from a foreign source; and we may reasonably connect it with the introduction of the knowledge of Persian forms of worship joined with the fiction of a happy or fortunate land known to the Sabæans who traded with India and Ceylon.

With respect to this paradise, the hoped-for rest of many thousands of Buddhists, the *sûtras* tell us that it is so called because those born in it have no griefs or sorrows; they experience only unmixed joys. "This happy region is exquisitely adorned with gold and silver and precious gems. There are pure waters with golden sands, surrounded by pleasant walks, and covered with large lotus flowers. Thus this happy abode is perfected and adorned. Again, heavenly music is ever heard in this abode; flowers rain down three times each day; and the happy beings born there are able, by going to other worlds, to wave their garments and scatter flowers in honour of countless other Buddhas dwelling therein. Again, there are in this paradise birds of every kind, peacocks, macaws, kalavinkas, &c., who during the six watches (*i.e.*, every four hours) raise their notes in concert to sing the praises of religion, hearing which there rises in the minds of the auditors remembrance of Buddha, the law, and the community. Again, the name of hell is there an unknown word; there is no birth in "an evil way," no fear of such births; and the birds that sing are but apparitional forms, made on purpose to sound the praises of religion. Again, the trees and strings of bells (curtains with bells) in that paradise, when moved by the wind, produce sweet and enrapturing sounds; and, when these sounds are heard, thoughts of religion rise within the minds of all the auditors. For what reason then is that Buddha called Amitāyus? Because the length of life (*āyus*) of that Buddha, and of those born there, is illimitable (*amita*); therefore he is so called. And why is he called Amitābhas? Because the splendour (*ābhās*) of that Buddha is illimitable. And living there is a multitude of purified and venerable persons, difficult to count, innumerable, incalculable. And, therefore, all beings ought to make fervent prayer for that country. They require not to have good works as their qualification; but only let them keep in mind the name of Amitāyus, and with thoughts undisturbed for one, two, three, four, five, six, or seven nights, treasure and repeat the name; then, when death draws nigh, this Buddha, with a company of saintly followers, will stand before them, and there will be perfect tranquillity. Therefore, let every "son and daughter" pray to be born in that Buddha-country." And so the account goes on, and the paradise of Amitābha extolled. It is difficult to describe the strong hold this belief has taken on the minds of the Buddhists in China. The repetition of the name of Amita is considered so meritorious, that believers in this strange myth go on incessantly repeating it, counting their beads, till the ear wearies of the sound Amita Buddh! Amita Buddh! There is an anecdote, however, told by I-tsing, of a priest of this school, which will show the effect of such a belief in rather a favourable light. It is told of a contemplative priest called Shang-tih. "This man," he says, "longed for the joys of the western paradise, and, with the view of being born there, he devoted himself to a life of purity and religion [reciting the name of Buddha]. He vowed to write out the whole of the 'Prajña-sûtra,' comprising 10,000 chapters. Wishing to pay reverence to the sacred vestiges of religion, and so to secure for himself greater merit with a view to be born in that heaven, he travelled through the nine provinces [of China], desiring wherever he went to labour in the conversion of men, and to write copies of the sacred books. Coming to the coast, he embarked in a ship bound to Kalinga. Thence he proceeded to Malaya, and there embarked in a merchant ship to go to Mid-India. Being taken in a storm, the ship began to go down, and the sailors and merchants were all struggling together to get aboard a little boat that was near. The captain of the ship, being a Buddhist, was anxious to save the priest, and called out to him with a loud voice to come aboard the boat, but Shang-tih replied: 'I will not come—save the other people.' And so he remained silently absorbed, as if he were satisfied to die. Having refused all help, he joined his hands in adoration, and, looking towards the west, he repeated the sacred name of Amita, and as the ship went down these were his last words. He had a follower who remained by his master and perished with him, calling on the name of Amita."[1]

[1] "Journal of the R. A. S.," October, 1881.

CHAPTER XIII.

RITUAL SERVICES OF KWAN-YIN.

§ 1. It has long been supposed that India must have been permanently affected by the presence of a Greek kingdom in the neighbourhood of its north-west frontier. Alexander the Great, we are told, was accompanied by some 3,000 artists and actors, who belonged to Hellas [1] —and the introduction of the new comedy into India is traced directly from Alexandria to Barygaza (Baroche) and thence to Ujjayinî (Ujjein) and North India. The plays of Æschylus and Sophocles were read at the Parthian court,[2] and the relationship between Parthian and Western Asia was a very close one. The Parthian prince, Pacorus, was, as Josephus tells us, in possession of Syria and at Jerusalem.[3] The close connexion of Parthia with India and the northern invaders (the Yue-chi) at this time has already been referred to. Then again, the marriage of Chandragupta with a daughter of Seleucus, and the apparent knowledge possessed by the grandson of Chandragupta, the great Asoka, with the Greek King Antiochus, and his embassy to four other Greek kings,—all this shows that there must have been some connexion between India and the western world, from

[1] Plutarch, "Alex.," 72, quoted by Ernst Windisch, "Der griechische Einfluss im indischen Drama."

[2] Darmetester, "Legend of Alexander."

[3] "Wars of the Jews," book i., cap. 13.

the time of the establishment of Greek influence in the valley of the Oxus. We read again, after the fall of the dynasty to which Asoka belonged, viz., the Moriya, of a persecution of the Buddhists in India by Pushyamitra, whose son, Agnimitra, met the Greeks in battle on the banks of the Indus. The Greeks soon prevailed, however, and under Menander, about 150 B.C., their conquests were extended to the Ganges. It was with this Menander, probably, that the discussion occurred known in Pāli as the Milindapañho, or dialogues between King Milinda and the Buddhist sage, Nāgasena. This book, probably written first of all in Sanscrit and translated into Pāli, exists in China under the title of "Questions of Nanda." It is occupied with discussion on certain abstruse points of philosophy, such as the existence of a personal self, the character of Nirvāna, &c., sufficient, however, to show that these questions interested the minds of the Greek conquerors, and led to inquiries and examination.[1] Then we have the evidence of coins, especially those relating to the prince called Gondophares, and his successors. With respect to these, I will quote General Cunningham ("Archæological Survey of India," vol. ii., p. 59). "The coins of the third class, viz., those of the Sacæ and Massagetæ Scythians, which belong to Gondophares and his successors are found chiefly in Seistan, Kandahār, and Sindh, and in the South Panjāb. The coins of

[1] M. Trenckner has published the Pāli edition of this work. He considers it to be a translation from Sanscrit. He says it is evident the original work cannot be older than the second century B.C.

Gondophares are found also at Kabul. Guided by these, I conclude that Gondophares was the founder of a Scythian dynasty whose proper territories were confined to Seistan, Kandahār, and Sindh. This is confirmed by the fact that Gondophares is almost certainly the same as Gondoforus of the early Christian legends, who is said to have put St. Thomas to death. Now, in the 'Legenda Aurea' Gondoforus is called the king of India—a title which agrees with the recorded accounts of the scene of St. Thomas's mission in Parthia, Persia, and India. But the place of his death is even more distinctly stated by Bishop Sophronius, who says, 'dormivit in civitate Calamina quæ est Indiæ,' which is further supported by the testimony of St. Gaudentius and the Roman Martyrology. An old inscription of A.D. 1070, on the door of the Basilica of St. Paul, on the Ostian road, also testifies that he was put to death in India. The Syriac writer, Amru, says that his tomb was in the island of Meilan, in India, but it is doubtful whether this is intended for the city of Calamina, which was the scene of his death. I feel inclined to identify this city with Min-nagar of the 'Periplus,' which may have been called Kara-mina, or black mina, to distinguish it from the older city of Min in Sakastene. Taken together, these statements are sufficient to show that King Gondoforus of the Christian legends was almost certainly the ruler of Western India in the time of St. Thomas, and, as King Gondophares of the coins was the ruler of the same country about the same time, we are, I think, justified in concluding that the two kings were the same person. I would assign the establishment of the dynasty of Gondophares to about 30 A.D., and the death of the founder to about 60 A.D. During this period the rule of Gondophares must have extended over the Eastern Panjāb, as I have found his coins in Multân and in all the old ruined mounds to the South of Lahore." The old legend concerning St. Thomas and his visit to India is thus confirmed by the existence of coins bearing the very name of the Indian king, of the legend, who reigned over the Indus district of north-west India at this very time. It is curious that among the Chinese books recently discovered there is frequent allusion to a Gandha, or Chanda, king, who belonged to the Indo-Scythian tribes that invaded India just before the Christian era. The word Gandha is a tribal title, equal to Chandana or, perhaps, the Greek Κοίρανος.[1] In any case, the fact is placed beyond reasonable dispute, that a King Gondoforus reigned in India at the time indicated above, and that communication was then so frequent and easy with this territory that the Apostle St. Thomas is believed to have been sent there for the purpose of erecting a house for the monarch, and that he died as a martyr and was buried in the city of Calamina, probably near the present Tatta (Patala) on the Indus. The opening of the legend in the Caxton edition of the "Aurea Legenda" is as follows :—

Saynt Thomas whâ he was in Cezaree,
Our Lord appiered to hym and sayde,

[1] But probably *Gandha* refers to Kanishka, as King of Gandhâra. The Greek Κοίρανος is a corrupt form of Gushan, a tribal name.

The kynge of Ynde gondeforus
Hath sent his provost Abanes
For to seke men that can wel the craft of masons.
And I shal sende the to hym.
And saynt Thomas saide,
Syre ! sende me overal sauf to them of Ynde.
And our lord sayde to him
Goo thy way theder surely for I shall be thy kepar.
And when thou hast converted them
Of Ynde thou shalt come to me by the crowne of martirdom.
And Thomas said to hym
Thou art my lord
And I thy servant
Thy wyll be fulfylled.
And as the provost went through the market
Our lord said to hym
Yong man what wilt thou bye,
And he said my lord hath sente me
For to brynge to him some that be lerned
In the science of masonrye
That they myght make for hym a palays
After the werke of Rome.
And thenne our lord delyvered
To hym Saynt Thomas th' appostle.
And told to hym that he was moche
Expert in that werke.
And they departed and saylled
Til they cam in a aste [city]
Where the kynge made a weddynge
Of his daughter, &c.

And then the legend proceeds with the marvellous story of the "botyller" who smote the Apostle for not eating and drinking as the rest, and how he was torn of dogs, and the hand that smote the Apostle brought into the assembly by one of the dogs. And then how the "yong man" that was married was blest by the

Apostle, and how there was found in his hand, after the Apostle had gone, a palmful of dates and so on.

We may, at least, conclude that when the "Aurea Legenda" was put together there was a tradition received in the church that St. Thomas had preached in India, and was buried there. It is remarkable that at this time, viz., about 50 A.D., was living a Buddhist writer called Asvaghosha, and that he was taken by one of these Scythian kings, an immediate successor, as it seems, of Gondophares, to North India, and is described as the personal adviser of the king, Chanda, or Gandha. His writings still survive in a Chinese form, and when examined will probably be found to be much tinged by a pseudo-Christian element. The present is not a proper place to enter largely into this question. I have translated elsewhere some of the writings of this Buddhist patriarch; but there is one book, the "K'i-sin-lun," or, "treatise for awakening faith," which has never yet been properly examined, but, so far as is known, is based on doctrines foreign to Buddhism and allied to a perverted form of Christian dogma. It will be found, I am convinced, that at this time there was an infusion into Buddhist doctrine of foreign elements derived from contact with Syria and its neighbourhood, which affected Northern Buddhism in a marked degree. It is suspected that some such intermixture of ideas and ritual occurred at a later period in Tibet, after contact with Roman missionaries, and it is equally probable that a similar fusion of foreign religious doctrines took place when the Christian dogma and ritual were first carried to the east by the Apostles and their successors.

Such a mixture may be traced, with some degree of certainty, in the forms of worship, adopted at an early date, paid to Kwan-yin. These forms of services were, in all probability, imported or introduced from Alexandria, or by the route of the merchants' trade from Alexandria and South Arabia. I have already alluded to the communication between Sabæa and the island of Socotora with South India. The merchants who traded with this district also visited the ports named in the "Periplus," among which Barygaza, the present Baroche, was the chief, and also Supâra, in the Konkaṇ. We have a list of imports and exports given us by the anonymous author of the "Periplus." All accounts tend to show that relations between this coast and Arabia and Egypt were regularly kept up. We can hardly suppose that there was no inquiry made about religious questions by the merchants who travelled through India down to the ports, who left records in the western caves, as *e.g.*, at Kârlê, "gift of Sihadhaya, a Yavana from Dhenukâkata"; of Dharma, a Yavana from Dhenukâkata; at Nâsik, "the Yavana Indrâgnidatta of the northern country." These Yavanas were Greeks of some sort. Wherever Dhenukâkata was, it was probably on the coast between Baroche and Bombay, and here these Yavanas had an establishment for trade. Just as the Sabæans had settled in Ceylon, so these Greek-speaking merchants had taken their residence at the western ports and carried on a regular trade with Arabia and Egypt. Ptolemy and the author of the "Periplus" both speak of the trade-route from Bharoch to Paitham and Tagara; and to quote the words of Dr. Burgess, the archæological surveyor of Western India, we can hardly doubt that the Yavanas trading from the coasts of Persia and the Red Sea got further inland than Kârlê and Nâsik. Indeed, we have the name of Indrâgnidatta, a Yavana from the north country, from the town of Damtâmitrî, probably a form of Demetrias, a town mentioned by Isidorus of Characenus, as in the neighbourhood of Kandahār, inscribed as a donor to the cave temple at Nâsik. This evidence, therefore, seems to show that the trade-route from North-west India, opened with Syria on the one hand, also extended to the sea-coast on the other; and thus the circle of communication was completed between Egypt and India by sea, and between Baroche and Supâra (the Σωφῆρα of the LXX) through the north-west provinces, and thence to Antioch on the Orontes, by land.

In the western Buddhist caves, especially those at Ajantâ, there are representations (paintings) relating both to Ceylon and to Persia. But the most curious and interesting for our present purpose are those paintings which relate to Kwan-yin or Avalokitesvara. We find what is called the "Litany of Kwan-yin" pictured there. This litany is a sort of prayer for deliverance addressed to Kwan-yin by those in distress. We will give a translation from the Chinese of the circumstances under which such supplications are offered:—

All hail, great compassionate Kwan-yin!
Though I were thrown on the Mountain of Knives

They should not hurt me!
Though cast into the lake of fire,
It should not burn me!
Though hurled down into hell,
It should not hold me!
Though surrounded by famished ghosts,
They should not touch me!
Though exposed to the power of devils,
They should not reach me!
Though changed into a beast,
Yet should I rise to heaven!
All hail, compassionate Kwan-yin!

Now, we are told that among the paintings in Ajantâ are representations of these very calamities, and Kwan-yin, being invoked, is drawn as coming to rescue her suppliants from their misery. We cannot avoid connecting this with the worship of the Sabæan Al-makah, "the hearer," introduced into Ceylon, and from Ceylon probably into Western India, by the merchants or traders who were residents or regular visitors at these places. But the step from the worship of such a beneficent being as Kwan-yin to a corrupt form of Christian ritual would be an easy one, and such is to be traced in a service of Kwan-yin still to be found and still practised in China. In this service, which is called the confessional of Kwan-yin possessed of a thousand arms and a thousand eyes, *i.e.*, the all-powerful and ever-watchful, there is a sequence of parts strongly resembling a corrupt form of the early Christian liturgies. In the preface to the service, the Emperor Ch'eng Tsu, otherwise called Yung Loh, the third emperor of the Ming dynasty, states, "that he has heard that Avalokitesvara [Kwantseu-tsai] Bodhisattva, urged by his infinite compassion, has engaged himself under a great oath to become manifested in every one of the innumerable worlds, for the purpose of saving the creatures who inhabit them." This is a wide-spread belief respecting the character of Kwan-yin. Hence, he is supposed to have gone down to the lowest hell for this same purpose; and, as this will illustrate the entire subject, it may be as well to notice the account as it is given us in one of the Buddhist *sûtras* first of all. The work is called the "Káraṇḍa-vyûha," or arrangement of the basket of Avalokitesvara's excellences. It opens in the way adopted from very early times, as if it was delivered by Ânanda, the personal attendant of Buddha, and who introduces his sermons by the phrase, "thus it was heard by me." He then proceeds to describe the occasion of the sermon he is going to record, and then proceeds: "When the vast assembly was met together, suddenly beams of light issued forth in the hell Avîchi." This hell of Avîchi is the lowest or deepest of the places of suffering, styled by the Chinese Buddhists "earth-prisons"; in the language of China it is termed *wu-kan*, without interval, *i.e.*, a place in which torments are endured without interval of relief. The account then proceeds to state that the beams of light reached the hall of assembly where Buddha was about to preach to his disciples, and "decorated the whole place." The pillars appeared to be inlaid with gems, the staircases to be covered with gold, &c. On this, one of the leading disciples stood up, and, having laid one shoulder bare, and bent his right knee to the ground, he put his hands to his forehead, and turned reverentially to Buddha, and addressed him thus: "I am filled with excessive wonder, O holy one, whence come these rays? Of what lord [Tathâgata] are they the visible majesty?" On which Buddha replied: "This is not the majesty of a Tathâgata [*i.e.*, of a Buddha]. O noble youth, the glorious Bodhisattva, Avalokite*s*vara, has entered into the great hell Avîchi, and, having delivered the beings there, is entering the city of the demons [*pretas*, hunger-stricken ghosts]; hence it is that these my rays have been emitted." Then the same disciple addressed Buddha in these words: "O holy one! What beings are found in Avîchi? Does he preach the law there where no joy is found? Whose iron realm, surrounded by walls and ramparts, is, as it were, one uninterrupted flame, like a casket of flashing jewels? In that hell where there is a great wailing cauldron, wherein myriads of beings are thrown; just as beans or pulse rising and sinking in a pot full of boiling water, so do these beings endure corporeal pain in Avîchi. How then, O holy one, does the Bodhisattva, Avalokite*s*vara, enter there?"

Buddha replies:—"O noble youth! just as an emperor enters a garden full of all precious things, attended with all his royal pomp, so Avalokite*s*vara enters the hell Avîchi; but his body undergoes no change. When he approaches the hell it becomes cool. Then the guards of Yama [the sovereign of hell], bewildered and alarmed, begin to think: What is this inauspicious sign which has appeared in Avîchi? When Avalokite*s*vara enters there, there appear lotus-flowers large as chariot-wheels, the cauldron bursts open, and within that bed of fire a lake of honey is manifested. Then Yama's guards, seizing all manner of weapons—swords, clubs, javelins, &c., and all the defensive armour of hell,—repair to Yama, the lord of justice, and address him thus :—'Let our king know that our "field of action" is destroyed and is become a place of pleasure, and is filled with all joy.' Yama replies :—'What is the reason thereof?' On which the guards answer: 'Let our lord know that an inauspicious sign has appeared in Avîchi. All has become quiet and cool, and a man assuming all shapes at will has entered there, wearing matted [twined?] locks and a diadem, and decked with divine ornaments, with his mind excessively benevolent, and like an orb of gold. Such is the man who has entered, and immediately on his entrance lotuses have appeared as large as chariot-wheels, and the cauldron has burst open, and within that bed of fire a lake of honey is manifested.' Then Yama reflected : 'Of what god is this the majesty?'"

Yama then proceeds to reflect as to the character of all the gods, but finds no one to correspond with the majesty of Avalokitesvara. Casting his eyes back, the ruler of hell beholds the visitor, and forthwith advances to worship him. Having delivered the sufferers in hell, Avalokitesvara proceeds to alleviate the torments of the famishing *pretas*—those wretched beings with forms like burning pillars (red-hot pillars), tall as skeletons, with mouths like needles' eyes, are delivered by his mercy. "The city becomes cold, the thunderbolts cease, and the door-keeper, with uplifted javelin, his hand busy with poison, his eyes red with anger, suddenly begins to feel the influence of mercy. Then Avalokitesvara causes cooling rivers to flow, and to cool the tongues of those suffering creatures."

Finally, they are all born in paradise (Sukhâvatî).

Such is the character of the oath of this imaginary merciful being, even as we read in the *sûtra* just alluded to, where Avalokitesvara says: "I am visiting the innumerable hells in the universe, resolved myself not to grasp the perfect knowledge of a Buddha until all beings have been, not only delivered from punishment, but are settled in the world of Nirvāna."

This being the character of the oath undertaken by Kwan-yin, the emperor then proceeds to say, "that for the purpose of securing this condition of salvation or deliverance, Avalokitesvara has formulated certain sentences, or mysterious words, which, if properly repeated, will render all creatures exempt from sorrow, and render them capable of attaining supreme wisdom. And, therefore, he adds, we bring this service and these words to the knowledge of our subjects immersed in the affairs of the world and not acquainted with this mode of salvation, and we earnestly exhort all men carefully to study the characters of this work and faithfully to follow them."

The service (which the writer has witnessed) begins with a direction as to the preparation of the altar of the merciful one. And here we must notice how this idea of "mercy," as the leading feature of Kwan-yin, is in agreement with the attribute of the Sabæan, or Himyaritic, "Al-makah," and was adopted afterwards by Mahomet as the chief characteristic of God. In arranging the temple, the image of Buddha is to be placed on an altar on the south side of the building. The figure of Kwan-yin must be put on an altar in the west of the building. This figure may be either one with ten arms, or six, or four, or two. [The "arms" represent the number of faces, which, in the first place, were intended to represent the all-looking (*samanta-mukha*) character of this being; but the phrase, being perverted to a literal sense, was symbolised by the actual number of arms and hands, which appear so gross and offensive in connexion with this idolatry.] On the day appointed for the recitation of the service (the 7th, 14th or 15th, 21st, and 28th of the month), in the morning early, the sacred precinct, within which the worshippers are to say the words, is to be defined. This is done by the use of a marked line, made with a knife and accompanied by the repetition of certain words. Then pure water is sprinkled towards each quarter, *i.e.*, at each corner of the precinct, then clean incense-dust is sprinkled on the floor, and afterwards a silken cord, composed of threads of five colours, is passed round the limits of the sanctuary, and the usual words repeated.

This having been done, the adjuncts of worship are arranged—lamps, incense, flowers, banners, and offerings of food.

The incense is to be made of the finest sandal-wood dust of the purest kind.

Then mats for kneeling, or stools for the same purpose, are to be arranged.

The "hours" are thrice in the morning and thrice in the evening (after noon),—the days those named before.

Before entering to worship, the brethren are to be careful as to personal cleanliness. If the garments worn are not new, they are to be the best in their possession. An hour before and after service there should be no "mixed conversation"; on meeting one another there should be only the customary respectful salutation. The mind should be chiefly occupied in considering the character of the "ten obligations" (*i.e.*, the ten vows of the order, not to kill, not to steal, &c.), before and after service.

If there be no real devotion during service, but only a confused way of going through an external duty, and if after it there be no right recollection, what benefit can be expected from these religious exercises?

The rules and directions for the service must also be carefully studied, so that in going through it there may be outward decorum as well as inward devotion.

Finally, let the worshippers (laymen) strive after a firm faith, and excite in themselves an earnest perseverance; and so, having purified the three faculties of thought, word, and deed, and engaging in the service in a proper way, they shall obtain their desires.

The "service" begins with a direction. These "directions" are printed in smaller characters than the rest.

"When the procession enters the great hall [the hall of contemplation—the 'temple'] they bow the head and pronounce this universal prayer (sentiment):—

"'Namo! great compassionate Kwan-shi-yin Bodhisattva.'"

[The expression "Namo" is generally translated

"Praised be," as, *e.g.*, in the sentence commonly found at the beginning of all Buddhist compositions, "Namo tassa Bhaghavato Arahato sammá sambhuddassa,"—"praise be to the blessed one, the holy one, the author of all truth."[1]]

Reciting this slowly and devotionally, let them enter the altar precinct, and having invested it three times successively, let them take their places in a standing position, and reflect thus:—"All the Buddhas are the same with myself; it is only because we are self-deceived that we think otherwise; to remove the obstacles in the way of such right knowledge, I now come to worship the 'precious objects,' and so desire to benefit all living things."

[From this, and the other explanations which follow, it is plain that, at the time when this service was composed, Buddhism had assumed the "mystic" form of belief known in the last stage of its development. In this period, all things were considered as one with the supreme; the cause of the illusion which leads us to think of subject and object (*năng* and *so*) being removed, there will be illumination; that cause is "ignorance" (*avidya*, not-seeing-ness).]

Now follows a hymn of incense: "Diffusive incense cloud! the brightness of holy virtue! [or, how bright is the character (*tih*) of the holy one!] Boundless is the heart of Bodhi! Wherever lights one ray [of that wisdom] there is worship [honour], there is praise. We look up and adore the king in the midst of the law!"

[1] "Khuddaka patha," a Pāli text, translated by R. C. Childers, F.R.A.S., vol. iv., part 2. N.S.

[The idea is here, that the canopy of the incense-cloud corresponds with the universal presence of the "heart of wisdom" (this is a euphemistic phrase for the "universal essence"). *Bodhi*, or wisdom, is supposed to be the one essence everywhere existing and diffused; as we recognise this, and learn such wisdom, we are made sharers in this "heart." "The king in the midst of the law," is another mystic phrase for the presence of Buddha, or the dharma-kāya representing Buddha, in the character of "the law." It approaches in one sense to a "religious" presence.]

Then repeat three times the following invocation :—

Namo ! incense-cloud canopy Bodhisattva.

[Here we see how the title, Bodhisattva, came to be applied to denote "a personification" of a quality. The idea of Kwan-yin was, in the first instance, the quality of "mercy." This quality was personified, and on account of its chief excellency the being representing it came to be considered as chief among the Bodhisattvas (saints). So in this invocation, the canopy of incense, representing the immanent presence of the "king of the law," *i.e.*, the presence of Buddha, in worship came to be personified as a Bodhisattva also.]

The invocation of incense finished, let (the officiating priest) say—

"Reverent and attentive !"

(Then chant the following.) (Bowing after each ascription.)

With all my heart I adore the everlasting Buddhas of the ten regions !

With all my heart I adore the everlasting law of the ten regions!
With all my heart I adore the everlasting "order" [congregation] of the ten regions.

(Then continue)

[Let] "This entire assembly, on their knees, reverently holding flowers and incense [or perfumed flowers] offer them as a religious offering."

Then let the assembly kneel, and, holding in their hands incense and flowers, let them chant the following:—

Oh! may the cloud of this incense [or the sweetness of these flowers] spread abroad and fill the worlds of the ten regions. Through every earth of all the Buddhas may it be perfected as a boundless incense-glory; fulfilling the way of a Bodhisattva, may it attain to the incense of a Tathâgata!

[It is plain, that in this there is nothing but mysticism. The cloud of incense being personified as a Bodhisattva, is expected to reach to the mystic condition of a Buddha.]

Then let the congregation (the professors of religion, *hing-che*) light their incense and scatter their flowers, and then with their entire heart repeat the following mentally.

I scatter this incense and the sweetness of these flowers far and wide [through the ten regions].
To represent the brightness of the mysterious [presence or doctrine of Buddha),
[Symbol of] The music of the heavens and the precious incense of the *devas*,
Their heavenly food and precious robes.
Not to be understood is the dust [the nature] of the mysterious law.

Every grain of dust [*i.e.*, every part of the incense] proceeding from the whole,
So every part [grain] proceeds from the whole law.
Circling round without impediment, it constitutes a glorious [body];
Spreading abroad through the universe, it reaches to [the presence of] the three precious ones,
And to the three precious ones throughout the mysterious worlds of the ten quarters.
So this offering which I here present
Is offered thus throughout the universe,
In every place without hindrance or impediment;
And so the odour of the pious deeds done through endless time
At last shall spread through every world
And cause all creatures to return
And gain the birthless wisdom of our Buddha.

[The above is a sample of the transcendental aspirations of Buddhist worshippers, belonging to this latest form of mysticism. The hope is evidently of a final restitution. As the atoms of incense unite and form a cloud, so by our pious deeds, the odour of which is spread through all the worlds, are we brought back to a complete union with Buddha.]

(The service then proceeds)

"Let all be reverent!"

(The head priest having said this bows once.)

The congregation then reflect that the three precious objects of worship are separated from us only by our own impurity. If we cleanse our thoughts and words and actions, then they will be united with us and we with them.

Let them, therefore, chant,

With all our hearts we hail thee and worship, O Sâkya Muni, lord of the world!

Then consider that the object worshipped and the worshipper are but one; let the obstacles of impurity be removed and he will come and give us rest.

The service proceeds in this way, with similar invocations to other objects of worship and similar reflections.

After the invocations, there is a prayer to Amitābha, and the other objects, finally to Kwan-yin. The prayer is of this character: "May the all-seeing and all-powerful Kwan-yin, in virtue of her vow, come hither to us as we recite the sentences and remove from us the three obstacles [of impure thought, word, and deed]."

We shall now merely give the succession of parts, as the portion translated is enough to show the character of the whole.

After the prayer of incense, except on the first day, the service proceeds with an introductory prayer to Kwan-yin. After this, there are ascriptions of praise to all the Buddhas and Bodhisattvas.

Next follows the lesson beginning thus—

> The *Sûtra* saith, &c. :—

After this, the litany of earnest request in this way—

> All hail, compassionate Kwan-yin!
> May I soon acquire perfect knowledge!
> All hail, compassionate Kwan-yin!
> May I soon attain divine wisdom!

Then follows the act of faith—

> Though I were cast on a mountain of knives,
> It should not hurt me.
> Though thrown into a lake of fire,
> It should not burn me, &c.

Then, after ten invocations to Kwan-yin, repeated quickly, and ten to Amitābha, the officiating priest continues with a second reading from the books, recording the vow of Kwan-yin to deliver all living things.

Now follows the repetition of the "sacred words," mostly in Sanscrit, not understood by the priests or people, but supposed to have a magical effect and bring deliverance by their inherent virtue.

After the repetition, there are various prayers of confession and strong aspiration after deliverance.

Finally, a further invocation, a procession round the altar, a prayer for "all that lives," and an ascription of praise; after this the assembly leaves the sanctuary.

It must be evident from a consideration of this outline of the service, that it is framed on a foreign model. It is opposed to the original creed of Buddhism, in which there can be no objective worship or real prayer to a superior power; and the character of the ritual, the succession of parts, and the language of the various portions, has nothing in keeping, so far as is known, with any Buddhist service elsewhere. In the southern school, so far as we can gather, the chief and most solemn service is the bi-monthly repetition of the Pratimoksha and the assemblies held on festival days, when the *Sûtras* are read, and sometimes the *Jâtakas*, or birth-stories, are narrated for the amusement of the people. The following is the Rev. Spence Hardy's account[1]:—

[1] "Eastern Monachism," p. 209.

"It is to be supposed that an atheistical system will pay little regard to acts of worship. The people, on entering the *wihâra* (*i.e.*, the chapel), prostrate themselves before the image of Buddha, or bend the body, with the palms of the hands touching each other and the thumbs touching the forehead. They then repeat the threefold formulary of protection, called the *tun-sarana*, stating that they take refuge in Buddha, in the *dharma*, and in the *Sañgha*, or they take upon themselves a certain number of the ten obligations, the words being first chanted in Pāli by a priest, or in his absence by a novice. Some flowers and a little rice are placed on the altar, and a few coppers are thrown into a large vessel placed to receive them; but no form of supplication is used, and the worshipper goes through the process with feelings kindred to those with which he would irrigate his field or cast his seed-corn into the ground, knowing that in due time, as a natural consequence, he will reap the reward of his toil. When special offerings are made, or a ceremony attended that is out of the common course, it is usually with the expectation of receiving some specific boon which may be relative either to this world or the next." This seems to be the usual form of daily worship in the south. In Japan—at least, in that part which the present writer visited in 1854–5—the Buddhist temples were daily frequented by the people. The usual course was to bow on entering, and then lay some flowers on the altar, and repeat some prayers kneeling. The women used to touch respectfully, and sometimes to kiss, the head of a red-lacquered figure of Ânanda, in recognition of their gratitude to him for gaining Buddha's permission to admit women into the community. After this, a few prayers were repeated, and the act of worship was over. In other cases, an assembly of priests was called and the *sûtras* read by one of their number, with some interruptions arising from interjaculatory utterances denoting either approval, or, as it sometimes seemed, the contrary. But only at the Hai-choang Temple, near Honan, was the service just referred to ever witnessed. And its peculiar ritual made a lasting impression on the present writer's mind. The service appears to be framed on the model of a Christian liturgy. Undoubtedly, there was a Christian Church planted at an early date in Malabar and Socotora.[1] We are told by Neander that, in the time of Constantine, a missionary, Theophilus, with the surname Judicus, is spoken of as coming from the island of Diu, by which is to be understood the island of Socotora. He stated that in Socotora and other parts of India which he visited from thence, he found Christianity already established, and that he had only to "correct certain things." We know also that the ancient Syro-Persian Church, "whose remains survive to the present day, boasts as its founder the Apostle St. Thomas, and pretends to be able to point out the place of his burial. Were this a tradition handed down within the community itself, independent of other accounts, we should not be inclined to yield credence to it; but neither, on the other hand, should we be warranted in rejecting

[1] Neander's "Church History," vol. i., p. 114.

it altogether. It is not impossible that this church, the earliest notice of which is found in the reports of Cosmas Indicopleustes, about the middle of the sixth century A.D., owed its existence to a mercantile colony of Syro-Persian Christians, and, having brought with it the earlier traditions of the Greek Mother-Church, might have simply transmitted these, but after a time the channel from whence they were derived was perhaps forgotten." Such is the opinion of Neander. It is well known, however, that there is a Malabar liturgy, and of this Dr. Neale says: "The Malabar liturgy I have never been able to see in the original, and an unadulterated copy of the original does not appear to exist. Diligent inquiry, but in vain, was made for it in India by the late Dr. Mill. As it is now printed, it was revised by the Portuguese Archbishop of Goa, Alexis de Menezes, and the Synod of Diamper (1599),—a revision which, as even Roman liturgists allow, shows utter ignorance of Oriental liturgies."[1]

And now with respect to the Buddhist service, it was brought to China during the Tang dynasty, *i.e.*, after the sixth century, and appears not to have been translated, as we have it, until the Ming dynasty, that is the fifteenth century. The former date would be in agreement with the acknowledged existence of a Christian church in Malabar. We observe, as points of agreement, that there is a prayer of entrance, a prayer of incense, an ascription of praise, lections, and then the recital of the "sacred words"; after this is a prayer against temptation, and a confession and dismissal.

[1] "Translation of Primitive Liturgies," p. 17.

It is unnecessary to dwell on the subject at greater length. Enough to have shown that this form of Buddhist worship, which exists in China, is probably derived from an accommodation of parts derived from foreign, and perhaps Christian, sources. The idea of Kwan-yin itself being extraneous to the Buddhist belief, it is not surprising to find the worship which is paid to her also derived from a foreign source.

§ 2. We cannot avoid referring, in conclusion, to the probable interchange of ideas between the early Gnostic writers and the Buddhists of Western India. It will be enough, perhaps, to state that the tradition respecting Adam's foot on the Sumanaketu, in Ceylon, comes to us first, as far as is known, through an obscure allusion found in the "Pistis Sophia," presumably a work of Valentinus. Speaking of the mysteries to be found in the book of Jeû, that is of Adam, he says, "this book is placed on the rock Ararad, and that one Kalapatanroth was appointed to guard this book, he who was at the top of Skemmut, where was the foot of Jeû." This is supposed to refer to the trace of Adam's foot, the idea being taken from the Buddhist tradition respecting the impression left there by Buddha of his foot. If so, it shows that the writer of the "Pistis Sophia" was acquainted with the story, and therefore probably with the legendary history of Buddha himself. It is plain, from a survey of his work, the "Pistis Sophia," that there is a Buddhist tone prevading the whole. The descent of Pistis Sophia into the lower world and into hell; the bright rays of her person; the plan of her recovery, and other particulars, are very similar to the myth of Kwan-yin. The thirteen *αἰῶνες*, corresponding to the thirteen heavens of the Buddhists, the character of the "unbounded" (*amita*), and the general plan of the conversation between the actors in this singular work,—all lead to an impression that there was a general knowledge of the later Buddhist literature spread beyond India, even as far as Alexandria and Egypt. We now pass on to make a few remarks on the worship given to Amitābha, generally regarded as the father of Kwan-yin, or Avalokitesvara.

CHAPTER XIV.

AMITĀBHA.

THIS being, as before stated, represents "the eternal," or the infinitely-glorious. The usual method of venerating him is by the repetition of his name. In China and Japan there is a school called the "tsing tu," or "pure land" school of Buddhists, who place their reliance on the virtue of this name for securing them birth in the western paradise. The name "Amita" is repeated incessantly, and the beads counted in connexion with the repetition, until the sound becomes wearisome. Regarding this kind of worship, or invocation, the books say: "Every person desirous of invoking this Buddha should first of all excite in himself a believing heart. By means of this invocation we obtain endless happiness. If a man has no faith, his exercises will be all fruitless. Therefore the *sûtra* says, 'Faith is the first requirement for the man who enters on the practice of religion.'" Again, we read, "If there be a virtuous man, or a virtuous woman, who has heard the name of Amitābha mentioned, and who, with firm purpose, retains the name and recites it [repeats it] for one day, or two days, or for seven days, with undivided heart [attention], without any confused thoughts, this man, when about to die, shall behold Amitābha with all his saints appearing before him, and he shall pass away to be born in that most blissful paradise called Sukhâvatî."[1] There is a large amount of native literature, especially in the south of China, relating to this form of belief. Among other popular expositions of it, one particularly attracted my notice. It is the representation of Amitābha under the character of one who "draws as by a rope" (*tsee yin*) (viz., to the repetition of the name of Buddha), and so secures for the virtuous man a birth in the western region. There is a picture of Amitābha standing on a lotus flower (the symbol of birth in his paradise), and with a rope in his right hand. On his breast is the figure of another lotus, and in his left hand his *pâtra*, or alms-dish. The rope is connected with a ship under full sail, evidently crossing the sea to the blissful paradise. It is full of male and female disciples. The ship is called "the boat of knowledge and love"; on the flag is an inscription, "The world of supreme bliss" (Sukhâvatî). There is a pendant flag on the bow of the boat, on which is inscribed "He who draws to the western region." At the post of command is a figure, with an exact representation of a mitre on his head, giving directions and overseeing the crew and passengers: he is probably Kwan-yin. On the sail is the following legend written:—"The one word Mi-to [Amita] is the precious sword for cutting down the crowd of heretical opinions. The word Mi-to is the method for crushing down the

[1] "Catena," p. 378.

terrors of hell. The word Mi-to is the bright lamp which gives light in darkness. This is the ship of love that crosses over the sea of sorrow. This word Mi-to is the direct road for escaping the circle [wheel] of transmigration. This word Mi-to is the pleasant way to shake off the bonds of further birth and death. This word Mi-to is the secret power that perfects the character of the saint [*rishi* or *isi*, in Chinese, *sin*]. This word Mi-to is the divine elixir that leads to a thorough change of conduct [or to conversion] [*hwan kwuh*]. These six words are a perfect substitute for the 84,000 gates of the law [modes of salvation,—referring to the 84,000 sections, or words, of the original Scriptures of Buddhism. The six words are Na-mo-O-mi-to-fuh, *i.e.*, praise to Amita Buddha. There are other six words, also sometimes referred to in connexion with this form of belief or superstition, viz., Om-ma-ni-pat-nie-hum, *i.e.*, Om, mani padme, hum; but the reference in the passage before us is to the former sentence]; they are the knife that in a moment severs the 1,700 trailing creepers [tangled vine, or rattan sprouts]. This one word Mi-to, without any other, is sufficient in the snapping of a finger to transport to the western world [paradise]." There is another scroll, or legend, on the body of the paper, which is to this effect:—"Among the various expedients laid down in the sacred books as methods of salvation, there is none equal to this method of invoking the name of Buddha. This one method [or means] is called 'seeking to be born in the western world [paradise].' Again, it is called practising 'the pure land' method of religion. The superlatively happy land of the west is the pure land referred to, so called because it is the land of the pure Buddha. In all the *sûtras* of the twelve divisions of the sacred canon (Tripiṭaka, San-ts'ong), men are exhorted to return, and are led to this happy land. The 84,000 gates of the law all lead to this. This invocation of Buddha is the most excellent and incomparable method of deliverance. An old priest says, 'Other methods of learning are like the progress of a small insect up a high mount, covering one pace in half an hour; but practising this pure land method is like a ship running before a fair wind and tide, 1,000 *li* in a moment.' Once entering this paradise [western region], we are eternally safe; those in the highest state forthwith ascend the ladder of Buddha [*i.e.*, are in a direct way to perfection]; those in a lower state enjoy the highest bliss of heaven [*deva* heaven]. The reward, indeed, is very excellent; the method very easy. There is no inquiry here about rich or poor, about wise or foolish, about old or young, male or female, about lay or religious, about secular or ascetic,—all can practise this mode of religion. All are exhorted therefore, whether virtuous men or faithful women, everywhere to practise it. Only get faith and repeat this one word. Seek to be born in this paradise. If the whole mind cannot be given to this subject, owing to worldly engagements, then, by repeating the name of Buddha each day, 3,000 or 5,000 times, there will be abiding merit. But if not able to do this, then reading through this scroll, and making one prayer [vow] that you may be born there, or that your father or mother may be born there, or that your father or mother, if suffering from sickness, may recover and obtain increased happiness, or that they, or any of your relations, may obtain conversion. In either case, your prayer shall be granted, and your own merit be greatly increased."

It is needless to describe at any greater length the character of this belief in Amitābha. It is the prevalent form of Buddhism in many parts of China, and especially in the island of P'u-to; and the ease with which its rules are attended to, and the general admission of male and female, rich and poor, into the privileges it pretends to offer, secure for it a large share of popular favour. In another sense, this paradise is regarded as a figurative description of our moral nature pure and at rest. "Amitābha means the mind clear and enlightened. The rows of trees supposed to surround the material heaven represent the mind cultivating the virtues. The music means the harmony in the mind. The flowers, and particularly the lotus, mean the mind opening to consciousness and intelligence. The beautiful birds mean the mind becoming changed and renovated." "The object," Dr. Edkins observes,[1] "of this figurative interpretation of the western paradise of Amitābha was doubtless to redeem the Tsing-tu [pure land] school from the discredit into which it had fallen, by abandoning the Nirvāna in favour of a sensuous heaven. The original inventors of it must have had

[1] Edkins, "Chinese Buddhism," p. 198.

such a notion of it as has been given [viz., that of an imaginary heaven], but they did not try to prevent its being accepted as real by the ignorant and uninquiring." Hence the effort of the Yun-tsi school to restore the fable to its original mystic form.

We have thus regarded Buddhism in China as a form of religion implying faith and worship. It now becomes us to turn to the question, how far the groundwork of all this is laid in philosophy, and what are its characteristics in that aspect.

CHAPTER XV.

BUDDHISM AS A PHILOSOPHY.

THE ground of all the Buddhist speculation is laid in one fact, viz., the existence of sorrow, and the aim and object of all its rules and practice is to escape from sorrow. It will be needless to consider the steps which led the founder of this system to his conclusion, that there is nothing but sorrow in the world, but so we find the fact. The problem he proposed to himself was, how to escape not only old age, disease, and death, but birth also as the source of all. Hence his aim was to reach that state which admits of neither "birth nor death," and this he called Nirvāna.

How he set about the task to sap the source of sorrow in his own case we find distinctly stated in the books. He hoped to do so by reaching enlightenment: his method was not a new one. We are told, in one of the Indian *Upanishads*, of a youth, called Naciketas, in whom faith was awakened on seeing his father give away all that he had, and he inquired of his father, "to whom, then, wilt thou give me?" Then his father said, "I give thee to Death." Naciketas then descends to the kingdom of death. Yama, the god of death, does not see him, so he remains three days unhonoured in the realms of the departed.

At length he is perceived, and the god of death offers to grant him three requests. He makes two. The third is respecting the state of the dead, "of the far-reaching future and the world to come"; this, "Death" is reluctant to reveal, but at length he grants the importunate inquirer his request. "The two paths of knowledge and ignorance diverge widely from each other. Naciketas has chosen knowledge; the fulness of pleasure has not led him away. They who walk in the path of ignorance endlessly wander about through the world beyond, like the blind leading the blind. The wise man who knows the One, the everlasting, the ancient god who dwells in the depths, has no part in joy or sorrow, becomes free from right and wrong, free from the present and free from the hereafter." This is the aim, then, "to get knowledge." Buddha, in order to attain this knowledge, left his home, and, after vain inquiries from the philosophers of the day, determined to seek illumination in his own way and by himself alone. He accordingly repaired to a quiet spot not far from the village of Gayâ, near Patna, and there sat down by the river side to solve the problem of sorrow and its origin. For six years, or, according to the Pāli, for seven years, he continued the most severe fast, and, with his tongue firm against his palate, conquered all desire after food or gratification of appetite. But he found no answer to the problem; but, at length, finding his bodily strength failing, he resolved to seek another way. Having partaken of food, with his body refreshed, he changed his place of religious exercise, and took his seat beneath a tree since known as the tree of knowledge. It was there he found the answer to the problem. He traced all back to "ignorance," the blindness of nature; and this ignorance was caused by the senses, and the power of the senses by the clinging, grasping desire for existence. Do away with this cleaving to existence, and, in regular sequence, the power of the senses will cease, the magic coil will untwine itself, and the want of light, the ignorance of nature, will disappear, and there will be illumination. Then birth, old age, disease, and death will lose their power, and the final goal of emancipation will be reached. Concerning this professed illumination, a thoughtful writer of our own time has stated his belief that there is an element of historical memory in it. He says: "The coming of such a sudden turning-point in Buddha's inner life corresponds much too closely with what in all times similar natures have actually experienced under similar conditions for us not to be inclined to believe in such an occurrence. In the most widely different periods of history the notion of a revolution or change of the whole man perfecting itself in one moment meets us in many forms: a day and hour it must be possible to determine in which the unsaved and unenlightened becomes a saved and enlightened man; and if men hope and look for such a sudden, and probably also violent, breaking through of the soul to the light, they realise it in fact. . . . In the age of which the sacred writings of the Buddhists give us a picture—and we may add with probability in Buddha's own time—the belief in a sudden illumination of the soul in the fact of an internal emancipation, perfecting itself in one moment, was universally prevalent—people looked for this 'deliverance from death,' and told one another with beaming countenance that the deliverance had been found, people asked how long it was till one striving for salvation is able to attain his goal . . . to whom the masters replied, 'That if they trod the right paths they would apprehend the truth and see it face to face.'"[1] And all this is agreeable to the unanimous testimony borne by all the records relative to the search and successful end of the search after knowledge by the Sâkya youth who became Buddha. He saw wisdom face to face. This expression is rendered in Chinese by the phrase *Shing tau*, perfection of reason, from the Sanscrit *abhisambodhi*, seeing wisdom face to face. The records state that, with reference to it, it is a condition above human reason; it can only be rendered by one word—"inspiration"; it is the indrawing of light, or *bodhi*, from without, into consciousness. Although the two words *sambodhi* and συνείδησις are probably of independent origin, they yet bear some resemblance both as to composition and meaning. Whatever the character of *bodhi* was, it indicated "knowledge," and in after years at least it represented an actual force or power underlying all phenomena. The particle *sam* is identical with σύν. The condition of one possessed of *bodhi* is that of "the awakened,"—sufficient in himself, wanting nothing, possessing everything; "self-taught in this profoundest doctrine, I have arrived at superhuman

[1] Oldenberg, p. 110.

wisdom," this is the language of the fully-inspired teacher. It is impossible not to compare this language of the Buddha—and it is the boast also of every fully-perfected follower of Buddha—with the proud independence of the Stoic philosopher. He, too, coined the word συνείδησις, and he also boasted of his self-sufficiency, his calm perseverance, and his rigorous self-discipline. It is singular, too, that Zeno, the founder of the Stoic sect, should have been of eastern origin. Born in Citium, a Phœnician colony of Cyprus, he is called and styled the Phœnician. His one absorbing passion, we are told, was the study of ethics; "he was essentially a philosopher of intuitions." Indeed, the character of this philosophy is so plainly Oriental, that Dr. Lightfoot does not hesitate to say, "it was the earliest offspring of the union between the religious consciousness of the east and the intellectual culture of the west"; and though he would trace the connexion to Shemitic influences, it is not improbable, in connexion with many marked agreements between the two, that the inspiration of the Phœnician Zeno may be traced to influences at work in the further east, where the merchants of Tyre and Sidon were not unknown. At least, there is one singular point in this possible intercommunication that cannot be overlooked, and that is, that the same Antigonus Gonatas, king of Macedon, who attended Zeno's lectures in Athens, and upon his return earnestly invited him to his court, was the same Antigonus to whom A*s*oka, the patron of Buddhism in India, refers in his thirteenth Edict. Of this edict we have three copies; one from Kapur di Giri, one imperfect one from Girnar (Giri-nagara), and a third from Khalsi, and in each of these he alludes to five Greek kings, viz., Antiochus (Theos) of Syria, Ptolemy (Philadelphus) of Egypt, Antigonus Gonatas of Macedon, Magas of Cyrene, and Alexander II. of Epirus. Is it not likely that, if A*s*oka knew so well the name of Antigonus Gonatas, the latter knew something of A*s*oka; and, if so, would not a king who sought the company of Zeno, and listened to his lectures, have learned something from his knowledge of A*s*oka, the great patron of Buddhism, of the teacher who resembled Zeno in so many points, and who had already brought the empire to a profession at least of belief in his doctrines?

But whatever be the exact meaning of the word Sambodhi, it was this that constituted the enlightenment of the emancipated ascetic, and was the ground of his professed ability to teach others.

In considering further the doctrine of Buddha from a philosophical point of view, there are some preliminary questions to be answered which will, at the same time, tend to a proper exhibition of the whole subject. What then do we find from authentic sources in China as to Buddha's belief (1) in God, (2) in the existence of soul, (3) the character of the supreme good, or, "the hereafter."

CHAPTER XVI.

BUDDHA'S CONCEPTION OF GOD.

It will be readily acknowledged, from our point of view, that Buddhism is an atheistic system. There is no word for God in Chinese Buddhist writings. The expression which came into use in the developed form of the system, viz., "all the Buddhas," is a pantheistic phrase to denote the combined virtue o the innumerable Buddhas supposed to exist throughout space. To understand this, and to give a satisfactory answer to the question we have proposed for ourselves to answer, it is necessary to examine the process by which the idea of God was excluded from the mind of the age in which Buddha lived, and especially from his mind.

This process was one we will venture to call of attenuation. When the first wave of the Aryan settlers came into India they brought with them certain beliefs in the Nature-powers, which they had personified under various names, and which they worshipped. We find that this first body of settlers were gradually pushed eastward by fresh immigrants, and the knowledge they professed, or rather the form of belief they held, remained stationary for ages. In this quiescent state it became intermingled with certain ideas derived from primitive tradition respecting the constitution of the world, which resulted in the formation of a Kosmical system, embodying opinions relating to the "upper world," and its occupants. These were objects of worship, and it was by a process of refinement or attenuation that Buddha the Teacher through these objects reached his idea of the highest condition of being which he called Nirvāna.

We must briefly sketch out the character of this cosmogony.

BUDDHIST COSMOGONY.

The lower world in which we live consists of four continents or great islands (*dvipas*), which are surrounded by a salt ocean. These islands or continents are placed in the four quarters or cardinal points. The southern continent, or *dvipa*, is called Jambudvipa, or the continent of the Jambu tree, because at the northern extremity of the land grows a great tree of this name, under which is abundance of gold. Within this sea, approaching to a centre, are various circles of rocks, they are seven in number, called by different names; we shall only notice the name of the outside one of all, the seventh,—this is called, in its Chinese dress, "the earth-holding mountains" (*Chi-ti-shan*). The original form was probably *Gandhâra parvata*, where *gan* is an old root for earth, corresponding with the Greek γῆν. If this be so, we might suppose that the idea of such a range of mountains was the common heritage of the undivided Aryan race. At any rate, such a supposition is not wholly improbable, if we consider next that in the centre of the world, as a navel or *umbilicus* of the earth, the Buddhists place the great mountain they call Sumeru—the Persian or Zend Alborz, the Greek Olympus, the abode of the gods. This is not the place to consider the origin of this word Sumeru; but it seems to be related to the old root *Sume* or *Suma*, which denotes the highest region of the firmament, or, "the heavenly water." The old belief, then, framed probably by the mountain races who dwelt in the cradle of the human race, perhaps in the high land of the Pamir, was that there were circles of rocks enveloping a central peak which was unapproachable, and therefore the residence of the gods; beyond these circles was the sea. We now find certain names given to beings of a super-human character supposed to inhabit the base of this unapproachable mountain, the strong-hand, probably a name for the sun, who in the Homeric Pantheon is also regarded as the lowest of the divine or super-human powers[1]; the chaplet-holder, probably the moon; above these, "the ever-wandering" or "the free," denoting the planets. Here we seem to have the oldest forms of pre-historic belief and worship. The sun, moon, and stars were also venerated by Shemitic tribes and others. The worship probably stretches back to the very earliest date of man's religious history. It is impossible to know what period of time it covers; but we find these names placed at the bottom of the list in the cosmogony of

[1] See "Transactions of the Royal Asiatic Society," July, 1877, p. 215.

the Buddhists. But another period sets in with the location of a certain number of gods on the top of this celestial mountain of Sumeru. There are thirty-three such beings, among whom *S*akra is chief. The Buddhist records state that these thirty-three powers represent the year, the four seasons, and the twenty-eight days of the lunar month. We know, at least, that the form of worship following the early reverence paid to the sun, moon, and stars, was that given to time (Saturnus; *annus* and *anna*). The transition was an easy one from the mere nature-emblem to the power which held these bodies in government. Time was supposed to control the movements of the bodies, which, in fact, marked the time supposed to be their ruler. There are notices of the thirty-three gods of Sumeru in the Veda or Vedic mythology; their origin, however, is not the same as in the Buddhist records, but the fact of the antiquity of the idea of such a number of imaginary deities on the summit of this mountain is confirmed by the agreement. The actual existence of such personified powers was accepted without inquiry in the primitive world. The Greeks really believed in the personal existence of Zeus (the bright sky) and of Here, the evening gloom (personified under the figure of the moon), and the morning breeze and the dawn, &c., as much as the Aryans of India did in *S*akra or Indra, or the Asvins, or the Adityas; and for ages or generations both in Greece and India such a belief remained as the best that could be offered the people. But, as in Greece so in India, a process of refinement began and went on among thinking minds, till an open rupture occurred. What Xenophanes did in Greece, Buddha did in India, only much more completely. It was probably during the period of repose, when the second wave of Aryan settlers, the Pañcâlas and Kurus, had taken quiet possession of the western province of India, that the process of refinement went on. First, there was a division made of the heavens placed above Sumeru. The "world of desire" occupied four tiers of heavens; the heaven in which there was no desire, but yet outward form, occupied five tiers higher up; and at last four heavens in which there was no visible form were placed above these. In all these heavens, however, there was a possibility of recurrence to lower grades of being, and therefore, there was no final emancipation or deliverance found in them. All these heavens were rejected by Buddha as insufficient for final escape—escape not so much from existence as finite existence. He, therefore, rose higher in his speculation than even these speculative philosophers, who refined away the idea of heaven to a formless void in which there is neither thought or absence of thought. He would have no possibility of return, *i.e.*, return to birth in any shape or form. And thus he frittered away the idea of personal existence, and therefore of a living God; but yet it does not appear that Buddha denied the existence of gods of the people. *S*akra and Brahma both play a part in the Buddhist scheme, only they are not supreme, *i.e.*, they are possessed of "qualities" that limit their supremacy. There is a work, called "Fang-wang-king" in the Chinese collection of Buddhist books, which corresponds with a *sûtra* known in the south called "Brahmajâla." In this work there is reference made to the theory of Brahma being the supreme God. The passage occurs on page 9. It speaks of Brahma being born by apparitional birth in the heaven he occupies. His term of years had expired in the higher heaven from which he descended, and he was now alone. He desired that other beings should dwell with him, and at that moment another was born by apparitional birth from a higher state of existence. Then the idea sprang up, "I" made this being, and, in the other case, "he" made me. Hence the thought of maker and creator arose. In this feeble way the idea of God as maker is accounted for. The whole passage is so important for a proper exposition of this doctrine that I will give the translation from the Pāli, which is fuller and more precise than that in the Chinese copy of the work.

"At the destruction of the world, very many beings obtain existence in the Âbhassara Brahma loka (Chinese, O-wei-po-lo). [The Âbhassara Brahma loka is the sixth of that series (*i.e.*, in the second tier, the heavens "without desire"), the entire number being sixteen. The longest period of existence in Âbhassara is eight *kalpas*. The inhabitants of the Brahma worlds have bodily form, but not of that gross nature as to require the nourishment of food: they have spiritual bodies (note by Mr. Gogerly).] They are, then, spiritual beings, have intellectual pleasures, are self-resplendent, traverse the atmosphere, and remain for a very long time established in happiness. There is a time when, after a very long period, this world is reproduced [that is, after its destruction it is renovated]. Upon this reproduction, the Brahma world, called the Brahma Wimāno, comes into being [the Chinese gives Shang-hu-hung = above space], but without inhabitant. At that time, a being, in consequence either of the period of residence in Âbhassara being expired, or in consequence of some deficiency of merit preventing him from living there the full period, ceased to exist in Âbhassara, and is reproduced in the uninhabited Brahma Wimāno. He is there a spiritual being, having intellectual pleasures, is self-resplendent, traverses the atmosphere, and is for a long time in the enjoyment of happiness. After living there a very long time alone, being indisposed to continue in solitude, his desires are excited, and he says: 'Would that another being were dwelling in this place.' At that immediate juncture, another being, either on account of a deficiency of merit, or on account of the period of residence being expired, ceasing to exist in Âbhassara, springs into life in the Brahma Wimāno, in the vicinity of the first one. They are both of them spiritual beings, have intellectual pleasures, are self-resplendent, traverse the atmosphere, and are for a long time in the enjoyment of happiness. Then, priests, the following thoughts arose in him who was the first existent in that world: 'I am Brahmâ, Mahâ Brahmâ, the supreme, the invincible, the omniscient, the ruler, the lord of all, the maker, the creator; I am the chief, the disposer of all, the controller of all, the universal father of all. This being was made by me. How does this appear? Formerly I thought thus: Would that another being were in this place. Upon my volition this being came here. Those beings also, who afterwards obtained an existence there, thought: This illustrious Brahmâ is Mahâ Brahmâ, the supreme, the invincible, the omniscient, the ruler, the lord, the maker, the creator of all. He is the chief, the disposer of all things, the controller of all, the universal father. We were created by him, for we see that he was first here, and that we have since then obtained existence. . . . It then happened, priests, that one of these beings, ceasing to exist there, is born in this world, and afterwards retires from society, and becomes a recluse. Being thus a houseless priest, he subjects his passion, is constant and persevering in the practice of virtue, and by profound and correct meditation obtains that mental tranquillity by which he recollects his immediately-previous state of existence, but none prior to that. He therefore says: That illustrious Brahmâ is Mahâ Brahmâ, the supreme, the invincible, the omniscient, the ruler, the lord of all, &c. That Brahmâ by whom we were created is ever-during, immutable, the eternal, the unchangeable, continuing for ever the same. But we who have been created by this illustrious Brahmâ are not ever-during; we are mutable, short-lived, mortal, and were born here.' "

This is the account as it occurs both in the Chinese and the Pāli scriptures of the origin of the idea of a creating God. The Buddhists are unable to accept the truth, that creation is possible in the Christian sense; and therefore, though they do not, as it appears, deny infinite existence, or even eternal life, they cannot connect with it any idea of a personal character, or "of a conscious volitional agency without which the universe is nothing else than a great self-acting machine."[1] There are some curious observations, not always intelligible, however, on this subject in Asvaghosha's "Life of Buddha." They occur in the eighteenth *varga* of the fourth book[2]; the author is speaking of the conversion of Anathapindada, the friend of the orphans, v. 1,454: "Thus he attained true sight, erroneous views for ever dissipated, even as the furious winds of autumn sway to and fro and scatter all the clouds of autumn. He argued not that Îsvara[3] was cause, nor did he advocate some cause heretical, nor yet again did he affirm there was no cause for the beginning of the world. If the world was made by Îsvara, there would be neither young nor old, first nor after, nor the five ways of transmigration, and when once born there should be no destruction. Nor should there be such thing as sorrow or calamity; nor doing wrong, nor doing right; for all, both pure and impure deeds, must come from Îsvara. Again, if Îsvara deva made the world, there should be never doubt about the fact, even as a son born of his father ever confesses him and pays him reverence. If Îsvara be creator, men when pressed by sore calamity ought not to rebel against him, but rather reverence him completely as the self-existent. Nor ought they to adore more gods than one. Again, if Îsvara be the maker, he should not be called 'existing

[1] Dr. Carpenter. [2] Page 260 (Beal's translation).
[3] *Îsvara*, the word used for God.

by himself,' because he always has been making [others beyond himself]. But if he has always 'made,' then he is always purposing to make, and is not, therefore, in himself sufficient. But if he makes without a purpose, then he is like the sucking child; or if with a purpose, then he is not yet complete. Sorrow and joy spring up in all that lives; these, at least, are not alike the works of Îsvara; for if he causes grief and joy, he must himself have love and hate; but if he loves and hates, he is not rightly called self-existent. Again, if Îsvara be maker, all living things should silently submit, patient beneath the maker's power, and then what use to practise virtue? 'Twere equal then, the doing right or doing wrong. There should be no reward of works; the works themselves being his, then all things are the same to him, the maker; but if things are one with him, then our deeds and we who do them are also self-existent; but Îsvara [by hypothesis] is uncreated, therefore all things, being one with him, are uncreated. But if you say there is another cause besides this Îsvara, then he is not 'the end of all' [the sum of all], and therefore all that lives may after all be uncreated [without a maker]—and so you see the thought of Îsvara is overthrown."

This extract will show, that in the time when the writer of it lived Buddhism had assumed a decidedly atheistical form, at least so far as the denial of an intelligent creator is concerned. In the course of its further development it took another shape; although there was no creator, yet the nature of Buddha was the basis of all that exists; and this nature is a definite something. For example, in the comments on a Chinese life of Buddha, dating from the seventh century of our era, such passages as the following occur: "With respect to the pure and universally-diffused body of Tathâgata, that in its very character is incapable of beginning or end. And what is this body?—nothing else but the substantial basis of his apparitional form [*i.e.*, as a mortal Buddha], perfectly at rest and pure—everywhere diffused."[1] Again, in the following sections, the writer says: "What we call Tathâgata is only that which is the basis [*tai*, the substantial hypostasis] of the universe. No form can represent it; it is imperishable, unchangeable, immeasurable." And then he proceeds to show that the cause of his being manifested as a human being was his infinite love or compassion, which is the chief of his perfections or attributes. All this, of course, is the result of the growth of years, and is rather a proof of the despair of the system to supply a definite idea of a sufficient cause of what exists in the presence of the acknowledged office of Buddha as a teacher and saviour from that which is the one positive reality in the Buddhist dogma, viz., suffering. The necessity of some idea of an existing power or superior being corresponding with Buddha is shown by the fable afterwards invented, that he left his appearance, or a sort of presence, on the "Ling" mountain near Rāja-griha, where he might be seen and worshipped. There is a story in the Buddhist canon in China of King Ajâtasatru going there with his minister, Jiva,

[1] Shih-kia-shing taou, p. 1.

and offering jewels and costly gems to the appearance of Buddha revealed to him there. And we cannot doubt that this presence was believed in and worshipped in subsequent ages by faithful devotees such as Fa-hien, the pilgrim who himself records his visit to the spot under the belief that Buddha was there present. Yet this falls short of the idea of God,—far short; and we are left with the enigma unsolved, how there can be worship—as there is—and prayer addressed to one who is no longer in any intelligible way a living reality. "Let it be understood," says Dr. Edkins, "at the outset, that the individual, personal life of Sâkyamuni Buddha terminated at his death when he entered Nirvāna. Buddhism does not know Buddha as a personality now living, but as a once-powerful teacher, living in his writings and in his institutions."[1] It will be necessary to add a word respecting the images of Buddha, which in one sense are worshipped in his place. We are told by the Rev. Spence Hardy, that "the Buddhists of Ceylon have a legend, that in the lifetime of Gótama Buddha an image of the founder of their religion was made by order of the King of Kósala, and the Chinese have a similar story; but it is rejected by the more intelligent of the priests, who regard it as an invention to attract worshippers to the temples."[2] This image, doubtless, is the same as that referred to by the same writer a little further on as the sandal-wood figure made by the King of Kósala, and seen by Fa-hien (400 A.D.) at *S*râvastî. The account of the Chinese

[1] "Nirvāna, according to Northern Buddhism," by Dr. Edkins. [2] "Eastern Monachism," p. 199.

pilgrim is this:—"When Buddha ascended into the Trâyastrimshas heaven to preach to his mother, after he had been absent ninety days, King Prasenajita, of Kósala, desiring to see him again, carved out of the sandal-wood called Gosirsha an image of the saint, and placed it on the seat which he usually occupied. When Buddha returned and entered the Vihāra [chapel], the image immediately quitted its place and went forward to meet him. On this, Buddha addressed it in these words: 'Return, I pray you, to your seat. After my Nirvāna, you shall be the model of all images made by my disciples.' On this, the image returned to its place. This was the very first figure of Buddha ever made."[1] This is evidently a fable made up in after ages, possibly for the glorification of some celebrated figure made in India, and with a view to give the adoption of such "representatives of Buddha" an accepted authority. The fact of the story being known in Ceylon shows that it had gained general credence, and it may be set down as the probable cause for corresponding images being made. But yet even these images are not worshipped. Service or prayer is offered up in their presence, but not to them. The present writer frequently watched the religious proceedings of the temple worship in Japan, when resident at Hakodate. The images of Buddha were generally small, and almost concealed by vases of flowers and incense-vases placed on the altar. The prayers were often said at such a distance, or in such a position, as to make it difficult for the image to be seen. The answer given to the question,

[1] "Fa-hien," p 76.

"Do you worship the image?" was a somewhat emphatic "No!"—and the only account of the matter was, that images were used, but not as a necessary part of the worship of Buddha. So that not even in their idolatrous worship do the Buddhists acknowledge a supreme God, or the image of a god actually existing.

There is, however, a theistic sect of Buddhists in which the existence of a supreme God is taught. Mr. Hodgson has brought this before us in his account of the Buddhist sects in Nepal. One of the questions asked of his Buddhist friend was this, "Who is Buddha? Is he God, or the creator, or a prophet, or a saint; born of heaven or a woman?"[1] To which the following answer was given, "Buddha means in Sanscrit 'the wise'; also, 'that which is known by wisdom,' and it is one of the names which we give to God, whom we call also Adi-Buddha, because he was before all and is not created, but is the creator. *S*âkya Buddha [*i.e.*, the historical Buddha] is earth-born and human. By the worship of the real Buddha he arrived at the highest eminence and obtained Nirvāna. We therefore call him Buddha."

It will be seen from this how the system is inconsistent with itself. This form of theism probably originated from the refinement of the idea of "all the Buddhas," which came into vogue during the period of the lotus-teaching development. This idea was that worlds presided over by Buddhas are as infinite as the sands of an infinite number of Ganges rivers—in other words, that there are "infinite Buddhas";

[1] Question VII.

giving this a concrete form, the idea of one Buddha, Adi-Buddha, or one universally-diffused essence, was coined and accepted, and this intangible something was clothed upon with attributes and called God. But I am not aware that the thought ever took such concrete form in China. The infinite Buddhas are known, and a universal essence of *dharma* recognised, but not one God endowed with attributes and the creator of all that exists.

CHAPTER XVII.

ON THE SOUL.

It is well known that there is no Buddhist word for the soul, *i.e.*, a personal and individual self in the Christian sense. There is much said about the spiritual portion of our nature, and in Chinese Buddhist books the word *shin* is sometimes used to denote a sort of individual spirit; it is likened sometimes to a flame, sometimes to an occult principle, but never to a personal and enduring substance. In a work published by a present writer,[1] the following passage occurs taken from a popular Chinese Buddhist treatise. The subject is, "signs at the time of death." The writer states: "When a man comes to die, the bodily functions, with the mind, become clouded and dark; as in a dreamless sleep, there is a complete suspension of all active thought. There being no exercise of mind, there is no conscious reflection: and so there is no knowledge or discrimination. Still there is a 'clinging' to existence, and this is called the principle of 'birth and death.' At this time, according to a man's good works or bad works, this occult principle ascends or descends, and

[1] "Catena of Buddhist Scriptures," p. 41.

the body gradually becomes cold to the touch: hence it is the verse says :—

> If from the summit of the head, a saint;
> If from the eyes the flame departs, a god;
> A man, if from the heart; a *preta*, from the groin
> A dubious birth from out the knee-pan goes;
> And from the bottom of the feet, a birth in hell."

And there is another passage following this which also illustrates the subject: "According to the 'Avataṁsaka Sûtra,' a man at the last moment of his life sees indications of his future destiny. If he possesses a bad 'character' [not *soul*, but 'tone of life'], he beholds all the miseries attending a birth in hell awaiting him; he sees the infernal lictors, and their cruel instruments of torture; he sees the river of fire, the scalding boilers, the spiked hills, the razor-trees, every misery which he will have to endure. But if he have a good 'character,' he beholds the heavenly mansions, the *devas* and *devîs*, their palaces and gardens; and, though yet alive, he even now enjoys an antepast of future happiness."

There is much more to the same effect; but all this was probably derived from a foreign source. It comes in just when the "lotus-creation" theory occurs in Buddhist history, and seems to be a part and parcel of the Persian or Sabæan intermixture of theories which occurred after the development of trade on the western coast of India. For just as the good who die, according to the Iranian myth, are welcomed by Vohu manô,[1] or their own good conscience, and conducted

[1] Tiele, p. 176.

into the abode of song, the dwelling-place of Ahura mazda and the saints, so are the good Buddhists welcomed by Amita and his saints,—"drawn," as it were, across the bridge *chinvaṭ* by the rope of the "ingatherer" to Paradise. So also the wicked who sink down into the under-world to be tormented by the spirits of evil, according to the Persian story, correspond with the wicked who, according to the Buddhists, already, ere they die, behold the infernal lictors. Indeed, we can only explain a great portion of the later form of Buddhism by the intercourse with Persia and Sabæa to which reference has already been made. But in all this there is no recognition of soul as an identical, personal being; it is, on the other hand, denied. There remains, after the individual is dead, *i.e.*, the dissolution of the five constituents of personal being, only an effect which follows on or accompanies the cleaving to life that in the ordinary man remains undestroyed. The effect is re-birth; the character of this re-birth depends on the "deeds done," the "building-power" of the previous life or lives. The occult principle departs and constructs another house, but there is no distinct identity that is re-born.

This theory of the "not-I" occupies a large portion of Buddhist psychology. It will be sufficient, perhaps, to denote in a few words what it means and does not mean.

It certainly means that there is no conscious recollection of former states of existence naturally or necessarily possessed; such a knowledge may be arrived at by the exercise of supernatural powers, but not in the ordinary course of things. The principle of re-birth acts necessarily and mechanically, even the gods cannot alter it; in this way it approaches the decrees of "fate." There is a curious story occurring in one of the Chinese lives of Buddha which will show this as it is popularly accepted. The tale is of a certain man who, having no son, was induced by his relatives to pay reverence to a certain tree in the neighbourhood of Benares, with a view to propitiate the favour of the genius of the tree, who was supposed to possess the power of granting the prayers of those who thus venerated it, although, as the Chinese editor remarks, this was not so, for the fulfilment of the prayer was the sole result of previous deeds on the part of the suppliant. Accordingly, the wealthy nobleman, having first protested against such a foolish idea as that a tree had power to answer prayer, consented to try the experiment. He pursued, however, a novel way, for taking with him a number of men armed with hatchets and other instruments for cutting, &c., he proceeded to the spot where the tree grew and addressed it thus: "You tree! I have heard you have power of granting prayer, if then you will procure for me the birth of a son I will offer you every kind of present; but if you cannot procure this boon for me, I will cut you down, and root you up, and utterly destroy you." The tree-spirit hearing these words was greatly distressed, and thought thus with itself: "What power have I to give this man a son, all that depends on himself and his destiny; and yet men persist in saying that this tree in which I have taken my residence has power to do this or that, and he says he will cut down the tree unless his prayer is granted, alas! alas!"

The tree *deva* then resolved to go to the king of the gods and lay the case before him. Ascending to heaven, he fell down at *S*akra's feet and said: "Help me, O king of heaven," &c., on which the king of heaven (*tin chu*)[1] replied: "What power have I to grant such a boon? for all depends entirely on the individual merit [or, character] of the man in question. But I will examine what the character of his destiny is." On this, he finds that the request may be justly granted, and he desires a *deva* about to be born in the world to be born in the house of this nobleman.

This story shows the character of the Buddhist belief in renewed birth. It is a birth depending on destiny; and the destiny is the power of moral force, so to speak, to effect either a happy or unhappy reproduction of life.

But as to what this belief is *not*: it seems plain that the entire Buddhist scheme rests on the belief that good deeds bring happiness, and evil deeds misery, hereafter. Death is not annihilation. There is a power that cannot be changed or affected by any control or will that must reproduce another life; and *that* life, again, will reproduce itself, until the great end of Buddha's doctrine is attained—the extinction of desire or cleaving—which can only be effected by the way he lays down; and then there shall be no builder, and therefore no house built, no *karma* to cause the cleaving principle another home.

[1] This expression, *Tin chu*, for the king of heaven, or *S*akra, *i.e.*, Jupiter, shows its unfitness for our word God.

There is much said about this theory of the "not-I" in the life of Buddha by Asvaghosha. The thought of "self" (soul), according to him, is the origin of sorrow, and sorrow is the great evil of the world (v. 1,363).

"This thought of self gives rise to all the sorrows which bind the world as with cords; but having found there is no 'I' that can be bound, then all these bonds are severed. There are no bonds, indeed: they disappear, and, seeing this, there is deliverance. The world holds to the thought of 'I,' and so from this comes false persuasions. Of those who say there is an 'I' [soul], some maintain that it endures, some say it perishes [at death.] These two extremes are both most mischievous. For if the soul is perishable, then the fruit we strive for, too, will perish, and at some time there will be [to us] no longer a 'hereafter'; this is, indeed, a meritless [thankless] deliverance. But if they say the soul [I] is everlasting [not to perish], then in the midst of all this birth and death we see but one thing which endures [viz., space; all things else perish]; if this is what they call the 'I,' then are all things living, one and the same; for all have this unchanging self, not perfected by any deeds, but perfect of itself. If this be so, if such a self it is that acts, let there be no self-mortifying conduct; the self is lord and master—what need to do that which is done? For if this 'I' be everlasting, reason would teach, it never can be changed." And the argument continues much in the same way for several pages, all intended to show that there can be no individual soul, either perishable or eternal. This same assertion is found in the "Brahmajâla Sûtra," and is argued there also at considerable length, the aim and upshot of the argument being to show that the *attâ*, or individual self, has no independent existence; that the idea of such individuality is a fetter (a bond), and must be broken; that a necessary step towards the insight which Buddha claimed, not derived from sensation, but from direct intuition, was this knowledge of non-individuality, this overthrow of the *atta-vāda*, or soul-theory. We are reminded hereby of the objection found in the "Phædo" to the immortality of the soul, on the ground that the soul itself was but a harmony, which must perish with the destruction of the parts of the machine or instrument that produces it. So the Buddhists compare the body to a chariot, and the idea of soul to the name given it whilst its parts remain together in relative connexion; but when the several portions of it are separated, then the name, or the thing called "a chariot," disappears.

LATER BELIEFS.

2. How this primitive and fundamental belief gave way, in process of time, to a tacit acknowledgment of a principle, amounting to individuality, will be apparent from a consideration of the doctrine of a paradise in which happy souls are born and enjoy the eternal presence of the infinite Buddha and his saints. Yet, with all this, the doctrine of non-identity, or at least of unconsciousness of identity, remains as the belief of the great majority of Buddhists in China. It may, perhaps, be useful to refer to the present belief among southern Buddhists on this point, especially as it seems

that the same kind of argument is adopted among the contemplative Buddhists of China, as we find in the quotation about to be made. The passage occurs in the discussion, held at Pantura, in Ceylon, August, 1873, between the Buddhist priest, Miggetuwatte (Mohottywatte Gunananda), and the Rev. David Silva, a Wesleyan missionary. The former, in the course of his reply to Mr. Silva, says: "If, as the Christians declare, the *âtma* which proceeds to another world is an undying something, and not a mere cleaving to existence, which was the view held by Buddhists, then, what do the Christians mean by it? Has the *âtma* [the soul] any shape? Is it like an egg, a stick, or a fruit? If it were some substance that was meant, surely it would not be difficult to confine it by locking up a dying man in an air-tight chest. If the Christians fail to explain the exact nature of the *âtma*, that of itself is conclusive evidence to prove that there is no *âtma* that travels to another world." He then proceeds to remark, with reference to the difficulty of another being produced at death yet not the same, that the Buddhist confession was "*na ca so, na ca anno*," *i.e.*, that it was not the same being, but yet it was not another; and he repeats this assertion, "though the being who was produced in another world was not the same human being that walked this earth, yet it was not another; and it was, therefore, most incorrect to say that it was a different person that suffered in a future existence for the misdeeds done in this, or that the existence of a living principle was denied by them."[1]

[1] "Controversy," p. 18.

So it appears the Buddhists will allow this much, that a subtle principle, which is otherwise called a cleaving to existence, continues to exist in connexion with deeds done in former time, but that this principle does not amount to a personal and individual being or thing. The contemplative Buddhists in China have a similar belief. There is an anecdote told of a disciple, called Lew hae-yueh, asking his master, a priest of the White-cloud school (*pih-yun shan soĕ*), the following question:—"Your disciple's thoughts are ever confused and rebellious; I cannot keep them fixed. Why is this?" On which the master replied, "Who is it whose thoughts are confused and rebellious?" He answered, "Your disciple's." "And who is it," the master said, "that cannot keep them down?" On this, Lew looked one way and another in confusion, and was unable to answer. The master then explained that it was this idea of another self that deluded him: "'self is master of self'; know 'this master' to be yourself, and such thoughts will not trouble you, and this self is not the soul, but the vanishing connexion of parts, called by the name of Lew."

The belief of later Buddhists on this question of soul assumed another form. The word nature was now used to indicate the existence of an undying and unchanging principle possessed by all. Buddha, in the second book of a well-known work, called the "Ling-yen-king," shows to the Mahārāja Prasenajita the character of this "nature." "I will now explain," he says, "the character of this nature, which admits of neither birth nor death. When you were a little child, how old were you when first you saw the river

Ganges?" The rājā said: "When I was three years old my tender mother led me to the temple of Jivadeva, standing near this river, then I knew that there was a Ganges."

Buddha said: "Mahārāja, you say that when you were three years old you saw this river. Tell me, when you were thirteen years old, what sort of appearance had the river then?" The king said: "Just the same as when I was three years old, and now I am sixty-two years old I see no change in it." "And yet," said Buddha, "you have become wrinkled and white-haired. But, tell me, has your sight also become wrinkled and different to what it was?" The king replied, "No, lord!"

Buddha rejoined: "Although, then, your face has changed, the nature of your sight is the same! But that which changes is capable of destruction; that which changes not must be incapable either of beginning or ending [birth or death]. How is it, then, that together with the imperishable sight-power you possess, there is joined something that you allow is perishing and changing? and how is it, still more, that those heretics, Makhali and the rest, say that after death there shall be a clean end of all life?" The king, hearing this, began to believe that after death there would be further life, and, therefore, with all the assembly, joyfully received the assurance. Buddha then proceeds to show that this sight-nature, which is imperishable, is the same as the nature of Buddha, and so draws the assembly to the belief that there is an imperishable nature in all of us which must continue to exist, as it has had no beginning, but is identical with the being of Tathâgata himself.

We have thought it well to say so much respecting the Buddhist belief in soul, to show how far it is accepted and how far denied in the usual Buddhist expositions of doctrine. The practical result of all these speculations is, that amongst the common people there is a firm belief in the reward hereafter of good deeds and the punishment of evil deeds; and among the more philosophical or mystical class of Buddhists the belief amounts to a supposed necessity of bearing the burden of repeated births determined by the deeds or character, till we be all restored to the one nature which is ours even now, but clouded and hidden by ignorance and especially by the fetter of a (supposed) separate individuality.

CHAPTER XVIII.

THE FUTURE HOPE: NIRVĀNA.

So much has been said on the subject of Nirvāna, that little can be added to the information we already possess. Dr. Edkins, in a paper written for an Oriental Congress, has given us the following account of a conversation he held with a Buddhist priest sixty years of age, of good repute as a learned scholar, and reported to be the best-read monk in either of the eight monasteries which are found together in one nook of the western hills, ten miles from Peking. "Do you think there is a future life or not?" "We neither say there is or is not." "Do not some men at death become sheep, and others, horses?" "I do not say they will. There is one thing that is really important. It is good conduct, good morality." "Virtuous conduct," he added, "is the basis of all religion. As for dogmas, they are true for those who accept them." "What then of Nirvāna, is it death or something different from death?" "No," he said, "it is not death, for it signifies the absence of birth and death." "What is your view of the dogma of the non-reality of existing things?" "Things are proved," he said, "to be not real by their destructibility. You burn them, they are reduced to ashes. You say you are an Englishman: you think of England and you are there. There is no reality in your thought. You are deluded if you think there is reality in it." He was very distinct, Dr. Edkins continues, on the point that definite belief is a fault. It is sticking to form. It is "*cho yü siang*" was his expression. This is literally sticking to form. The moment you form ideas too pronounced on the existence of a future life, or the Nirvāna, or on the non-reality of existing things, you cease to become a consistent Buddhist.

This priest belonged to the Lin-tsi branch of the contemplative school of Chinese Buddhists. With them the essence of religion is quietism; to have no strong belief on any point except the necessity of virtue and good conduct,—the rest will adjust itself.

Referring to the books, however, we receive definite information as to the early and late belief of northern Buddhists on this subject of Nirvāna. It is spoken of as a deliverance consequent on destruction. So Buddha says: "After my Nirvāna, *wo-mie-tu-heu*," that is, after my body has been destroyed, and in consequence deliverance obtained. But what is the "deliverance"? The oft-repeated answer is—a deliverance from "birth and death" (*sing sse*). The truth is, so it would seem at least, that sorrow was regarded as inseparable from organised life, or from life as a separate item in any condition. And, therefore, without defining it, the primitive belief was that the supreme happiness was exemption from re-birth. Does not this contain in it the germ of the later Pantheism or spiritualism into which the system grew? For, if there is to be no birth, we must go back to the condition before birth began;

that is, as it seems, to the condition of the "Eternal one." Whether this word Nirvāna has not some reference to that condition of a non-breathing life, that is, of the Creator ere he began his creative work (as we speak), is not satisfactorily answered. It has been propounded as a possible explanation of the word, and if it could be borne out, the idea, at any rate, of Nirvāna would be brought to a determinate issue. For if, as the Buddhists say, we are possessed of the one nature of Buddha, and if by recovering this we reach our goal of perfection, then this perfection consists in going back to that nature ere it became deluded and darkened by ignorance. At least, the definition of destruction as a part of the formula for Nirvāna alludes to the destruction of every part of the being called "man." The bodily form, of course, but beyond that the faculties of perception (*vedanā*; Ch., *sheu*), consciousness or the receptive power of thought (*sangña*; Ch., *siang*), discrimination (*sankarâ*; Ch., *hing*), and conscious knowledge (*vijnanâ*; Ch., *shih*). So that, if these perish, it would seem that all must disappear, and the result be annihilation. But this is not so: for the result is described as deliverance from the fetters of existence; that is, from the bonds which constitute sorrow. Beyond this, however, we find in the developed form of the doctrine the positive assertion that Nirvāna consists in joy, permanence, personality, and purity. "It may be compared," Buddha is supposed to say, "to the absence of something different from itself. In the midst of sorrow there is no Nirvāna, and in Nirvāna there is no sorrow. So we may justly define Nirvāna as that sort of existence which consists in the absence of something essentially different from itself." Again, in another place, Buddha says: "I do not affirm that the six organs of sense, &c., are permanent, but what I state is that *that* is permanent, full of joy, personal, and pure which is left after the organs of sense and the objects of sense are destroyed. When the world, weary of sorrow, turns away and separates itself from the cause of all this sorrow, then by this rejection of it there remains that which I call the 'true self,' and it is of this I speak when I say it is permanent, full of joy, personal, and pure." So in the later speculation this thought is repeatedly brought out, that Nirvāna is a positive condition of unfettered bliss.

We need hardly dwell on this subject further. It might admit of an indefinite amount of discussion; but, for the purpose of this inquiry, it is enough to know that the theory of an annihilation of existence is not by any means an acknowledged explanation of the meaning of Nirvāna. The difference between the destruction of all elements of limited existence and the cessation of being is a distinct one and perfectly recognisable. It may be and is a baseless vision of the future condition, that it admits of no positive description; but yet, as it is full of joy, and pure, and permanent, and in a high sense a personal one, it affords a sufficient motive to what the Peking priest described as the basis of all religions,—correct and virtuous conduct.

CHAPTER XIX.

THE ETHICS OF BUDDHISM.

THE religion of Buddha is founded on correct life. This is his fourth truth: there is sorrow, and multiplicity of sorrow, there is a possibility of ending sorrow, and that is "the way" he taught. This way, or noble eightfold path, has been frequently described; let us take it as we find it in a Chinese work already referred to, viz., the "Buddhacharita," by the Bodhisattva, Asvaghosha. This book has the advantage of a fixed date, viz., about the middle of the first century A.D., and therefore gives us a terminus from which we may measure the growth of the system. At v. 1,243 we have an account of the first sermon he preached to the five men at Benares. "All sorrow at an end, I rest in peace,—all error put away. My 'true sight' greater than the glory of the sun; my 'equal and unvarying wisdom,' vehicle of insight; 'right words,' as it were, a dwelling-place; wandering through the groves of 'right conduct'; making a 'right life' my recreation; walking along the road of 'proper means'; my city of refuge in 'right recollection'; and my sleeping couch 'right meditation':—these are the eight roads, even and level, by which to avoid the sorrow of repeated birth and death."

This is the "middle path" marked out by Buddha. Those who walk along this road, he says, shall fall "neither on the one side nor the other," that is, neither on the side of an over-wrought asceticism, nor on the side of undue indulgence. The particulars relating to this eightfold way vary a little in the southern records, but the agreement is marked enough to show that this was the method laid down by Buddha for his first disciples. Instead of "right sight" we might substitute "right views," which includes in it, according to the Chinese explanation, the faculty of "discerning the truth," opposed to erroneous or false views. "Equal and unvarying wisdom," the second path, refers to correct thought and intent, *i.e.*, absence of evil or pernicious (in the sense of heretical) thoughts. "Right speech" is defined as the exclusion of idle or pernicious words or language. "Correct conduct," is explained as the practice of purity. "Right life" is the life of a religious mendicant. "Right means" is defined by Dr. Davids as "right endeavour,"—it seems to refer to the use of means for the conversion of others; perhaps "right expedients" would be a better term; Buddha is said to have used expedients in the character of his teaching adapted to the case of his hearers. On one occasion, when he was intent on the conversion of the wife of the son of Anâthapiṇḍada, a favourite disciple, he used a parable referring the particulars of a female's beauty to inward adornments, the ornament of "a quiet and gentle nature," and by these means brought her to a loving and obedient frame of mind. Again, when he was intent on the conversion of the Matangî girl (a low-caste woman) who had fallen in love with Ânanda, he said to her, "Ânanda is a priest and closely shaved, but you have comely locks upon your head; if you are willing to be shorn, then I will cause Ânanda to espouse you,"—accordingly she causes her mother to cut off her hair and returns. Then Buddha shows her that the Ânanda she loved was not his eyes, or his nose, or mouth, or body, but the real Ânanda was the grace of his religious life, on which, being already shorn as a priestess, she was converted, and was thus joined in mystic wedlock to her choice. These were the expedients used by Buddha adapted to circumstances, and it is to the use of these right means that the expression "*samyakupāya*," refers. "Right recollection" is the memory of the excellent law, in other words, the repetition from a true memory of the words of the law, the teaching of Buddha, and the formulæ of worship. "Right meditation" (*samâdhi*) is the proper exercise of mental abstraction, the whole mind in a true state of vacancy, *i.e.*, for the admission of a mystical apprehension of truth. These eight ways constitute the ground-work of Buddha's ethical system. The point is, by the practice of these moral rules, to reach the end of his doctrine, which is rest and freedom. In the present life, this end may be attained, salvation from sorrow is possible even now; but hereafter, when the body is dissolved or broken up, and the individual being at an end, then the deliverance is completed; it is called then "without remains," an unshackled state of existence, like the great Nirvāna of Buddha himself.

Undoubtedly, these eight paths or ways form the

earliest code of rules given by Buddha for the direction of his followers. There is, however, another ancient document containing the ethical principles of his doctrine known in China, and, so far as the present writer knows, not mentioned among southern books. This is a short work called the "Substance of the Vinaya," which is generally printed with the little work called the "Sûtra of Forty-two Sections," which was the first Buddhist book translated into Chinese (A.D. 70). It is probable that this is the text referred to in the Asoka edict of Bhabra, under the title "Substance of the Vinaya"[1] (*vinayasamākase = vinaya samākassa*, contraction or summary of the Vinaya. Rhys Davids, *op. cit.*, p. 225, n.): it is called in Chinese the "Sûtra of the Contracted Rules of the Vinaya" (*lioh-shwo-kiau-kiai king*). The same epitome of moral rules occurs as a sermon towards the end of Asvaghosha's "Life of Buddha." From this circumstance, taken in connexion with the other, viz., its being bound up with the "Sûtra of Forty-two Paragraphs," it is plain that the treatise is a primitive one, and therefore, as it bears the very name given to it in the edict, it is probably the "Substance of the Vinaya" which was extant in Asoka's time. I do not find the sermon in Dr. Davids' translation of the book of "the great decease"; it comes, however, in the northern version of that book, as we find it in Asvaghosha, immediately after the record of Subhadra's death. As this short treatise exhibits the character of Buddha's ethical teaching, I shall here produce a translation of it.

[1] Rhys Davids' "Buddhism," p. 223.

CHAPTER XX.

THE SUBSTANCE OF THE VINAYA.

BUDDHA, the first watch of the night being passed, the moon bright-shining, and all the stars clear in their lustre, no sound within the quiet grove, was moved by his great compassion to declare to his disciples the following testamentary precepts of his law. He therefore spake as follows: "After my decease, you ought to reverence and obey the Pratimoksha [rules for moral discipline] as if it were your master [*i.e.*, in my place], as a lamp shining in the darkness, or as a jewel carefully treasured by a poor man. The injunctions I have ever given, these ye ought to follow carefully and obey, and treat in no way different from myself.

"Keep pure your body, and your words, and thoughts; enter not on any business matters [affairs of trade]; have no lands, nor houses, nor cattle; store up no wealth of money, or of grain. Avoid all this, as you would avoid a pit with fire at the bottom. So neither cultivate the fields, nor cut down trees, nor practise arts of healing or of medicine. I forbid all star-gazing or astrology, forecasting lucky days or unfortunate events by signs, prognosticating good or evil.

"Keep the body temperate, eat at proper times,

receive no mission as a go-between, compound no philteries, abhor dissimulation, follow right doctrine, and be kind to all that lives; receive in moderation what is given, receive but hoard not up: these are, in brief, my spoken precepts. These form the groundwork of my rules; these also are the ground of 'full emancipation.' Enabled thus to live is rightly to receive all other things. This is true wisdom, this is the way: this code of rules hold fast and keep, and never let them slip or be destroyed.

"For when pure rules of conduct are observed, then there is true religion; without these, virtue languishes; found yourselves, therefore, well on these my precepts.

"Grounded thus, the springs of action will be well controlled, even as the well-instructed cowherd guides well his cattle.

"Ill-governed feelings [senses], like the unbroken horse, run wild through all the domain of sensuous objects, bringing upon us in the present world unhappiness, and in the next continual suffering. They land us, like the wild horse, in sure destruction; therefore, the wise and prudent man will not allow his senses licence. For in truth these senses [organs of sense, or appetites] are our greatest foes, causes of misery; for men, enamoured thus by sensuous things, bring back upon them all the miseries [they had escaped]. Destructive as a poisonous snake, or like a savage tiger, or like a raging fire, the greatest evil in the world; he who is wise is freed from these. What the wise man fears is this: a light and trivial heart, which drags him down to future misery; a ittle sip of pleasure, not looking at the yawning gulf.

Like the wild elephant freed from the iron curb, or like the ape that has regained the forest, such is the light and trivial heart: the wise man therefore holds and governs it. He who lets the heart [the inclinations] wander loose, that man shall not obtain Nirvāna [rest], therefore you ought to hold the heart in check, and go apart from man's society and seek a quiet resting-place [hermit's abode]. Know when you ought to eat and the right measure; and so with reference to the rules for clothing and for medicines; take care you do not, by the food you take, encourage in yourselves a covetous or a passionate mind. Eat food to satisfy your hunger, and drink to satisfy your thirst; just as we repair an old or broken chariot, or like the butterfly that sips the flower, but injures not its fragrance or its texture.

"The follower of mine [mendicant] should take good heed in begging food not to cause offence: if a man be liberal in giving, do not overtax his generosity; for 'tis not well to calculate too closely the strength of the ox, lest by working him [loading him] beyond just moderation you should cause him injury. Be diligent both in the morning and at noon and night to store up good works. Be not overpowered by sleep in the early night and morning, but in the middle watch with heart composed take rest and sleep; be thoughtful towards the dawn of day. Sleep not the whole night through, making the body feeble and relaxed, but rather watch and think,—when the fire shall burn the body, what sleep will then be possible? Who shall waken the body when death has seized his prey? The poisonous snake dwelling within the house can be enticed away by proper charms, so the black toad that dwells within the heart the early waker disenchants and banishes. He who sleeps carelessly [*i.e.*, without proper covering] has no proper modesty; but modesty is like a beauteous robe, or like the curb that guides the elephant. Modest behaviour keeps the heart composed; without it, every virtuous root will die,—without it, man is as the beast.

"If a man should cut your body with a sharp sword and sever limb by limb, let no angry thought or of resentment rise, and let the mouth speak no ill word. Your evil thoughts and evil words but hurt yourself and not another: nothing so full of victory as patience, though your body suffer the pain of mutilation. Remember! he who has patience cannot be overcome, his strength is strong indeed! give not way to anger, then, or to reviling. Anger and hate destroy religion, and, moreover, they destroy all dignity and comeliness of person: as when we die our beauty is effaced, so the fire of anger burns up the beauty of the mind. Anger is foe to all advance in the religious life [merit-field]; he who loves virtue, let him not be passionate. We may not wonder when the worldly man, oppressed by sorrow, yields to anger; but, for the 'houseless one'[1] to indulge in anger, this indeed is opposed to principle, as if in frozen water there were found the heat of fire.

"If indolence arises in the mind, then rouse yourself to go and beg, holding in your hand the begging-dish; on every side the living perish, what room for idle-

[1] That is, the religious mendicant.

ness? The worldly man, relying on his means and substance, who encourages within an indolent mind is wrong; how much more the religious man, whose purpose is to seek the way of rescuing others, who indulges indolence?—surely such a thing is hardly possible.

"Deceit and truth [crookedness and straightness] are in their nature opposite and cannot dwell together more than frost and fire. For one who has 'professed' religion and entered on the way of straight behaviour, a false and crooked way of speech is not becoming. False and flattering words are like the magician's wand; but he who ponders on religious truth cannot speak falsely.

"Covetousness brings sorrow; desiring little, there is rest and peace. To procure peace in life there must be small desire, much more for one who seeks eternal peace [salvation]. The niggard dreads the money-seeking man, lest he should filch away his property; but he who loves to give [has no such fear], his only fear is lest he should not have enough to give. We ought to encourage 'small desire,' that we may have to give to him who wants, without such fear. From this desiring-little mind we find the way of true deliverance; to obtain this, you should practice knowing-enough [contentment]. A contented mind is always joyful, this is the joy religion gives; the rich and poor alike, having contentment, enjoy perpetual rest. The rich, without contentment, endure the pain of poverty; though poor, a contented man is rich indeed!"

Without continuing this text, the sum and substance of it is evidently the recommendation of a pure morality, embracing temperance and moderation of mind and body, and also the virtues of patience, contentment, and charity.

Such is the teaching of Buddha, regarded from this point. The same rules are inculcated in another *sûtra* translated into Chinese about the same time as the one just named, and called the "Sûtra of Forty-two Paragraphs." Only to give one or two extracts from this book to illustrate the subject, let me quote the following:—(viii.) A wicked man who reviles a virtuous one is like a man who looks up and spits at heaven: he does not soil the sky, but himself. The virtuous man cannot be hurt; the misery that the other would inflict comes back upon himself. (xv.) A man who devotes himself to religion is like a person taking a lighted torch into a dark house: the darkness soon is dissipated and there is light. Once persevere in the search for wisdom and obtain the truth, what perfect illumination will result! (xix.) Buddha said: "Never tire of self-reflection; find out the inner *âtma* [soul or real self]; that which we call 'self' is but a passing guest, and its concerns are like the mirage of the desert. (xxvii.) Watch against unbelief! keep away from worldly thoughts, and exercise yourself in thoughts about religion, then you will reap the fruits of faith." (xxxiii.) There was a disciple who every night recited the Scriptures with plaintive and weary voice, desiring to show his sorrow for a thought he had entertained of returning to the world. Buddha calling him said: "When you were living in the world, what did you practise in the way of daily occupation?" He answered: "I was always playing on the lute [*vinâ*]." Buddha said: "If the strings of your instrument were too loosely strung, what was the consequence?" He said: "There would be no music." "And if they were too tightly strung, what then?" He replied: "The sound would be too sharp." "But if they were tightened in a middle way, what then?" He answered: "There would be universal harmony." "Even so," said Buddha, "keep your mind well adjusted in the middle way, and you will gain your end."

Without further quotations from similar works, we see that the ethical system of Buddha was founded on self-government and virtue. The method was in the use of moderation, neither asceticism on the one hand nor licence on the other; and the end was to attain present rest of mind, and freedom from all cleaving to worldly things, with a view to an eternal emancipation from renewed birth.

CHAPTER XXI.

THE ORDER.

LITTLE can be added to what has already been said with respect to the order, or Saṁgha, the congregation, of the Buddhist community. The rules for admission are the same in the northern school as in the south. A child of eight years of age, or as soon as he is old enough to drive away crows, may be admitted into the order as a novice (*shami*, *sâmanera*). He must, however, have the consent of his parents, and be free from physical disqualification. The word *Sha-mi* is defined in the Chinese "Daily Manual,"[1] as "ceasing from worldly occupations, and engaging in loving duties to all creatures." Both the *shami* and the *shamini* (*i.e.*, male and female novices) have to take the following vows:—(1) not to kill; (2) not to steal; (3) not to marry; (4) not to lie; (5) not to drink wine; (6) not to use perfumes, or flower-wreaths, &c.; (7) not to attend dances or theatres; (8) not to sit on high and luxurious seats; (9) only to eat at fixed hours; (10) not to possess cattle, gold and silver, or precious stones. The "Daily Manual," in commenting on these rules, says: "Drinking wine

[1] Page 16.

causes a person to lose control of himself; his guardian spirits [or good spirits] are grieved at such conduct, and when dead he falls into the hell apportioned for drunkards. Scents and flowers on the person produce libidinous thoughts. Music and dancing are opposed to modesty, and produce dissipation. These are the amusements of the world, not of religious persons. High and luxurious seats produce idle habits, and are not allowable. To eat at improper times refers to the rule only to take one full meal at noon. To be always wanting food is the great impediment in the way of deliverance from the bonds of life.

"To possess wealth and jewels is the root of covetousness; to get money and to desire to be always eating [*i.e.*, covetousness and gluttony] are the two first of the five evil desires. The rule is to eat in order to nourish life,—this is allowable; and for worldly men to possess wealth is allowable, but not for the 'religious.'"

At the age of twenty the novice [if he desires] may be admitted into full orders; he then takes upon him the 250 rules of the Pratimoksha. He must then also receive the tonsure and wear the robes.

He then selects the monastery in which he proposes to reside, and is admitted to the *saṁgha*, or congregation.

There are different rules of conventual discipline, according to the school to which the priest attaches himself. In the contemplative school, which has taken root in southern China, the chief duty is profound and continued meditation; the practice of external means is not so much employed. The founder of this school, Bodhidharma, was a native of South India, and came to China A.D. 526. He is spoken of as the twenty-eighth patriarch of the Buddhist church; this succession of patriarchs, however, is unknown in the Theravadî school of Ceylon. "He represents a school that despises books, and reduces Buddhist teaching to the simplest possible rules. He decried book-reading, and his system made the monasteries much more mystical and meditative than before."[1] This mystic school has kept its hold in southern China to the present day. There are two volumes of a work commonly met with in the Canton province, called "Shan-lin-shun-pih-shwo," or sayings of the Shan, or meditative school of priests, in which the opinions of these mystic Buddhists are largely quoted. Their one aim seems to be to acquire the "nature" of Buddha by giving up all active employment. This agrees with what we read of Bodhidharma, who, on arriving in China (it is sometimes said he arrived there on the leaf of the tea-plant), was invited to Nanking, where the emperor of southern China held his court. The emperor said to him: "From my accession to the throne I have been continually building temples, transcribing sacred books, and admitting new monks to take the vows: how much merit may I be supposed to have accumulated?" The reply was, "None." The emperor: "And why none?" The patriarch: "All this is but the insignificant effect of an imperfect cause not complete in

[1] Edkins, "Chinese Buddhism," p. 86.

itself: it is the shadow that follows the substance, and is without real existence." The emperor: "Then what is true merit?" The patriarch: "It consists in purity and enlightenment, depth and completeness, and in being wrapped in thought while surrounded by vacancy and stillness. Merit such as this cannot be found by worldly means." The emperor then asked: "Which is the most important of the holy doctrines?" To which the monk replied: "Where all is emptiness, nothing can be called 'holy.'" The emperor rejoined: "Who then is it that replies to me?" The patriarch: "I do not know."[1] This extract exhibits the character of the mystic school of Buddhism. It discourages book-learning; the attainment of perfection is the work of the heart—hence, we are not surprised to find the class of priests belonging to this school described as being imbecile in appearance and idle in their lives. It is the natural consequence of their "do-nothing" axiom. Bodhidharma himself, we are told, passed many years gazing at a wall, and was called the wall-gazing Brahman. He died finally of old age, and was buried in the Hiung-er mountains between Honan and Shansi.

The Tian-tai school of priests, on the other hand, allow the necessity of knowledge as well as meditation. This school was founded by Chi-k'ai, not long after the arrival of Bodhidharma in South China. He had left his home in Honan, and wandered to a romantic spot in the Cheh-kiang province, where he founded a monastery. It is called the Kau-ming

[1] Edkins, *op. cit.*, p. 102.

convent. It was, however, at a place called Si-tsoh, not far from the present Wan-nian monastery, that he composed the system of doctrine called "Chi-kwan," that has ever since distinguished his school. He had at first followed the doctrine of the contemplative school, but he was dissatisfied with it; he did not approve of the rejection of study or the teaching of the sacred books. He taught, therefore, the union of knowledge (*chi*) and meditation (*kwan*) as being the true means of enlightenment. I may be allowed here to quote what I have written elsewhere, concerning the teaching of this school[1]:—"The system of Chi-k'ai was founded on principles advocated in the 'Chung-lun,' a treatise written by Nâgarjuna Bodhisattva. This treatise advocates a middle way in the exposition of Buddhist doctrine; it rejects all antitheses, and endeavours to find the middle truth in the reconciliation of opposites. 'So,' Chi-k'ai said, 'the true secret of Buddha's doctrine is found neither in book-learning nor external practices, nor yet in sole attention to ecstatic contemplation; neither in the exercise of pure reason, nor in reveries of fancy; but,' he said, 'there is a middle course which includes all and rejects none'; this system he called *chi-kwan* [fixity (in learning) and meditation], in agreement with the saying found in the 'Dhammapada,' 'Without knowledge there is no meditation, and without meditation there is no knowledge; he who has knowledge and meditation is near Nirvāna.'" With regard to the school as it now exists, we have the testimony of

[1] "Catena of Buddhist Scriptures," p. 246.

a visitor, that the priests of the Kwo-tsing-sze, one of the establishments of the sect, in Cheh-kiang, are both numerous and respectable. The Superior was a middle-aged man, surrounded by a number of persons well-acquainted with the principles of Buddhism They maintained that all systems were alike, and all led to one result. As to image-worship, they said that the most advanced Buddhists worshipped without the use of any images: the middle-class used images in their worship as helps to devotion; and the rest used neither images nor worship. As for themselves, they could worship without any images at all, and they thought it best to do so. They were asked, What was the need, then, for images? They said they were necessary for the vulgar. The ground of this system is found in the stanza which Chi-k'ai places at the beginning of one of his books:—

> Scrupulously avoiding wicked actions,
> Reverently performing virtuous ones,
> Purifying the intention from selfish desire,
> Is the doctrine of all the Buddhas.

This verse is found in "Dhammapada," and represents a fundamental principle: "Do nothing wrong; do all that is right." The guide to determine the right and wrong is the moral teaching of Buddha, which is to be gathered from the books. The way to advance is, to meditate therein. There is a good deal said about this system of the Tian-tai priests in the book before quoted, and to that work the reader is referred.

The third school of Buddhists to which we shall

briefly allude is the Kiau-men, or school of learning or doctrine only. These Buddhists are opposed to contemplation as a means, and advocate attention to the literal teaching of Buddha found in "the books." They belong to the "exoteric" branch of the religion. Dr. Edkins, in speaking of this school, quotes from a native writer, who thus compares Buddha and Bodhidharma[1]: "Tathâgata taught great truths, and the causes of things. He became the instructor of men and *devas*. He saved multitudes, and spoke the contents of more than 500 works. Hence arose the Kiau-men, or exoteric branch of the system, and it was believed to hold the tradition of the words of Buddha. Bodhidharma brought from the 'western heaven' the seal of truth [true seal], and opened the fountain of contemplation in the east. He pointed directly to Buddha's heart and nature, swept away the parasitic growth of book-instruction, and thus established the exoteric branch of the system containing the tradition of the heart of Buddha. Yet the two branches, while presenting of necessity a different aspect, form but one whole."

Without enlarging on this point, we may allude to the little book called the "Daily Manual of the Shaman," as giving an account of the duties of the disciple adopting the teaching of this school as his guide. There are duties prescribed for every event of the day. On awakening in the morning, he must sit up in a grave posture and repeat a verse, to recall his mind to the duties of religion :—

[1] Edkins, *op. cit.*, p. 158.

On first awaking from my sleep,
I ought to wish that every breathing thing
May wake to saving wisdom.

On hearing the convent-bell calling to prayers, he ought to say:—

Oh, may the music of this bell, wherever heard,
Produce in all a sense of rest,
And quiet every care, &c.

On getting out of bed, say:—

On putting down my feet and standing up,
Oh, let me wish that every living thing
May gain release of mind and self
And stand upright in perfect rest!

On putting on the vestments, say:—

Assuming this my upper robe,
I pray that every living thing
Obtaining the true principles [of religion]
May safely reach the other shore.

And so on for all the duties, even the most trivial, of the day. There is direction given how to bow to a sacred object, how to read the *sûtras*, how to walk on the road when begging, and so throughout.

It is plain that this school must have considerable influence in keeping alive a healthy tone in a system otherwise full of the elements of decay; for mysticism, by itself, cannot endure; but when supplemented by action, or united with practical aim and duties, it may take its place in, and perhaps give a character to, the complex system which we call Buddhism.

THE TANTRA SCHOOL, OR THE PRACTICE OF CHARMS AND MAGICAL SIGNS.

The repetition of words not understood by the people has always taken its place, in the estimation of the superstitious, among religious practices, and in Buddhism it has obtained singular authority. This may be owing to the prevalence of such beliefs or customs among the northern nations that adopted Buddhism as their religion; or it may result from the natural development of Buddhist modes of thought. It is plain that, if there is no recognition of a personal and supreme being, and yet no distinct denial of a superior power or an occult principle that may be brought into harmony with our own being, the use of prayer can only be for the purpose of bringing into play a virtue residing in the act itself: the step from this to the belief in a virtue residing in the words is a very small one. We find, then, as the theory of a universal essence or force, or, as the Chinese love to call it, "heart," was accepted, so the use of words for adjusting the relationship between the subjective and this universal "heart" came into use.

In the service of Kwan-yin, to which reference has been made in the previous pages, the sacred part of the function, or, as we should say, "the mystery," consists in the repetition of the words. These words must be effectual, if properly repeated. This superstition has taken deep hold on northern Buddhists.

Every one knows how the magic formula of "Om mani padme hum!" is repeated in Tibet; and it is no less common in China. There is an instance of this in the inscription found on the limestone archway at Keu-yung-kwan, in North China. This archway stands about five miles north of the entrance of the Nankow pass. It is covered with mythological and symbolical sculptures, evidently of Indian origin. It is probably the bottom part of an old pagoda that was built "across the street," as it is still known by that name. This pagoda, we are told, though erected for the benefit of the locality, proved an object of such terror to the superstitious Mongols coming south, from their native wilds, that they could not be induced to pass under it; and so it was necessary, in the early part of the Ming dynasty, to remove the upper part of the pagoda, the policy of the government being to conciliate and attract these wild nomads. Several Europeans, who had passed that way, had noticed the village and the archway. Father Gerbillon, who was there on his way to Mongolia, in 1688, says: "The village might pass for a little town. The gate by which it is entered is like a triumphal arch"; and the Russian Timkowski, in 1820, says: "Here the road begins to be very difficult, especially for carriages, and does not change for a distance of five *verst*, as far as the fort of Kiu Young (*Kouan*), the principal defence of this passage. The interior of the middle gate is ornamented with figures of heroes sculptured on the walls." Mr. A. Wylie, however, was the first to draw attention to the inscription found on the archway, and in a paper read before the Royal

Asiatic Society, in 1870,[1] he produced the whole of it with a translation. Without introducing all of it here, we may select one or two sentences such as these: "Om! namo bhagavate! om bhûr om bhûr om bhûr om sodhaya, sodhaya, visodhaya visodhayasama," &c. The words are Sanscrit, but they are repeated by the people with no knowledge of their meaning. The translation of the first portion of the inscription is as follows: "Om! adoration to the holy Buddha, who art exalted above the three worlds —adoration to thee! which is equivalent to Om Bhûr om! Bhûr om! Bhûr om! Purify, purify, completely purify! O thou incomparable one, who embracest all space, and whose splendour has appropriated the sphere of knowledge! thou who art welcome of all the Tathâgatas, whose speech is blessing, and who art immortal, consecrate me by sprinkling me with holy water and the great *mudrâ* [the seal or sign made with the fingers] with the words of mystic prayer," &c. The inscription is mixed up with disconnected charm words, and if any meaning can be assigned to it, the object of the words is to produce a mystical purity and deliverance for all who repeat it aright.

In all the little manuals which occur in such numbers throughout China, similar mystic sentences are given as necessary for assisting the worshipper. Such phrases as "Om, lam! Svar! Seou li, seou li [srî, srî] Mo-ho seou-li," occur throughout their pages, used as invocations or magical charms for

[1] Vol. v., par. 1.

bringing the heart into union with the principle of being. It would be needless to produce other examples, as they are all of one character, and consist of broken, corrupt sentences, extracted from Indian books, and drawn up at a late period in the history of the religion. These sentences are called To-lo-ni (*dharāni*), and are used not only in the usual recitation of prayers, but on special occasions, such as the service for asking for rain. There is a special treatise for this purpose published by royal mandate in China, and called the "great cloud-wheel rain-asking *sûtra*." The preface to it was written so recently as 1780 A.D., by an emperor of the present dynasty, Kien-lung. The theory of compelling rain to fall is connected with the very old belief in the existence of dragons, or *nâgas*, who either withhold or grant rain according to their benevolent or malevolent disposition. Buddha revealed certain sentences which would have the power, when properly repeated, to overcome all evil influences and produce a good disposition among the *nâgas*, and so cause rain to fall. These sentences he delivered to the great dragon-king and they are recorded in the *sûtra*. They are like the rest: "Tan-chi-ta To-lo-ni, To-lo-ni, Yan-to-lo-ni San-po-lo-ti-sse-che, pi-che-ye," &c. These being repeated in the order given are supposed to have the power required; and they are so repeated by the Chinese.

But perhaps the most complete body of magic sentences to be found in any Chinese work are those which occur in a popular *sûtra* called the "Ling-yen-king"; and as a consideration of this work will illustrate the late philosophical character of Buddhism, perhaps this is a proper place to refer to it.

It has long been suspected, that the development of Buddhism led to the later forms of Hindoo superstition known as the worship of Vishnu, Siva, &c. There is much to support this opinion. We might refer to the account given by Hiouen Thsang, in the tenth book of the "Si-yu-ki," referring to the construction of the Brahmara convent by King Sadvaha, a patron of Nâgarjuna, a most distinguished Buddhist scholar. This convent, which was probably somewhere near Nagpore, was consecrated to Parvatî, under her name of "The Black Bee"; we are told that Brahmans and Buddhists lived together in its caves, until the latter were expelled by force by the former. What happened here occurred also at a celebrated convent called Nâlanda, in south Behar, about 30′ south-east of Patna. This monastery at one time held as many as 10,000 monks, forming the most splendid Buddhist establishment in India. It was celebrated as a place for study, both for Brahmanical books and those of Buddhism. In the end the two systems coalesced. Among other works originating from this establishment is the one called briefly by the name given above,—the Leng-yen-king,—but when written in full "Sheu-leng-yen-king," or "*S*urañgama Sûtra." It was brought to China and translated by Paramiti in A.D. 705. Now, on page 30 of the eighth book of this *sûtra*, it is stated, that "this volume was brought from India and belongs to the 'Kwan-ting' school." The school so named is, in Sanscrit, called the Mûrddhābhishiktas, or the "head-baptised." The explanation of this title given in the passage referred to is this, that those who hold the principles of this book, on them the wisdom of Tathâgata descends and washes the "head of the heart," just as the Kshattriya king is baptised at his consecration. This explanation is a plausible one, and may probably account for the custom of sprinkling water on the head commonly practised in Tibet, but only administered in China to high personages, who are thereby admitted into the Buddhist church and solemnly invested as protectors of religion. But there is another, and more probable, derivation of the term, as applied to a Buddhist school. We are told by Colebrooke ("Essays," p. 272), that among the mixed classes in India there is one called Múrdhábhishicta, which consists of those born from a Brahman and a woman of the Kshattriya class. Now, the application of this term to a Buddhist school seems to intimate the mixed character of the tenets held by those belonging to it, that they were Buddhist and Brahman intermixed: and such is the character of the book we are considering. Its principles are these, that there is but one universal soul, which by a sort of inversion is conceived of as multiplied, but only in error; that this is the one "ever-quiet yet ever-shining" reality; that we and all that lives are one with it. By removing the dust from the mirror all is clear; so by removing false and inverted thoughts about ourselves from the heart, we are restored to our one and true condition. The subject is illustrated in many ways, but to mention only one: Buddha desires to show that our ideas of multiplicity are a delusion, he therefore takes a soft and embroidered handkerchief, and in the sight of the congregation tied in it a knot, then, showing it to Ânanda, he said, "What call you this Ânanda?" He answered: "It is called a knot." On this, Buddha repeated the act, and tied a second knot above the first, and asked again, "What call you this?" They replied again: "This is a second knot," and then he repeated the same thing and the same question until six knots had been tied. Buddha then addressed Ânanda and said: "When I first tied the handkerchief you said it was made into a knot; yet the handkerchief itself is one piece of silk: how then can you speak of a second, third, and fourth knot as distinct from the first and the handkerchief?" On this Ânanda replied: "Lord! this valuable embroidered handkerchief, originally woven from silken threads into its present form, although in itself essentially one substance, may, when tied up into knots, be spoken of as knotted, even if there were a hundred knots: on what ground then does Buddha demur to the name?" Buddha addressed Ânanda: "You allow, with respect to this embroidered silk, that in its original character it is but one; but when I tied each successive knot you said it was each time a distinct knot: you should, therefore, clearly understand the nature of this inquiry, that substantially [essentially] this silk handkerchief is one and the same, but that accidentally [by circumstances] it is called by the name of each successive knot. Now then, tell me what you think: Each knot I tied down to the sixth you told me was a different knot. I propose now to undo this sixth knot: do I thereby affect the handkerchief as one, or the remaining five knots?" Ânanda replied: "No! lord, the last knot is different from the first, and yet the handkerchief remains the same." "So is it," Buddha said, "with your six organs of sense and the great unity. If you keep the knots tied, there must of necessity rise the thought, 'This knot is this and not that,' so the question of this and that is raised. If you want to get rid of this thought, all you have to do is to tie no knots, or untie them all, you will then have the same handkerchief without knots—so is it with the senses. From the first, your mind and nature being in disorder and confusion, there has arisen a false excitement of a knowledge derived from sense *e.g.*, from sight, and this knowledge wildly exercised has produced endless deceptions: at last, worn out with excessive action, the sight has caused the belief in objects of sense, as the eye fatigued sees in space fanciful objects, figures, and sky-flowers. But really in the depth of the *true* sight-power there lies no cause or ground for this deception; thus from excess of action have sprung up as qualities and characteristics of this false appearance the ideas of worldly phænomena, mountains and rivers, the great earth, death, and Nirvāna; these all alike are but perishing qualities (*siang*) of a conditioned existence."

Ânanda said: "The excessive action and confusion of which you speak I take to correspond to the tying of the knots: tell me then how to get rid of it." Then Tathâgata, with his hand, taking the knotted handkerchief, smoothed out the left part of it, and said: "Is it now untied, Ânanda?" To which he answered, "No." Then the lord, shaking out the other part with his hand, smoothed it to the right, and said: "Is it now untied, Ânanda?" To which he answered, "No!" The lord then added, "I have smoothed the silken napkin out, on the right and left, and yet you say it is not untied: tell me then, how is it to be unloosed?" To which Ânanda answered: "You must take the middle part, the heart of the knot, then separate each part, and it will come untied." Buddha replied: "Good! good! Ânanda, if you wish to untie the knots [and make all smooth] begin at the heart."

By this enigmatical method Buddha is supposed to exhibit the non-reality of qualities or distinctions, and to show that the mode of recovery is by undoing or doing away with the inversions or delusions of sense. In order to accomplish this, we must begin at the heart; and to get the heart right and the delusions corrected, he imparts to his followers a long series of sacred words or charms by the repetition of which the end will be reached. These *dharāni*, which will be found in the seventh book, are 427 in number, and consist of Sanscrit words, including the objects of common Hindoo worship—such as Parvatî, Narayana, Kuvera, and so on—conjoined with the names of the Buddhas and the sacred books. So that here we find the idea fully developed, of the power of words, whencesoever derived, to govern the heart and produce magical effects. These *dharāni* are explained in a fanciful way in a work published at Canton in the twenty-seventh year of the reign of Taou-Kwang (A.D. 1848), the fourth month, the eighth day. Each syllable is restored to its true sound, and the whole put together so as to appear to make some sense. It is plain the priest who undertook the task did not understand his work, for he gives us the most random explanations of ordinary Sanscrit words. It is enough for us, however, to gather that the use of these charmed words was introduced into Buddhism at a time when the system was losing its distinct character from connexion with Brahmanism.

It will be plain, from what has been said, that the practical teaching of Buddha has been to a great extent effaced in China by the later growth of Pantheism and mystic fancies. The "heart" is regarded as the substantive basis of all things, and to get this heart, or heart of Bodhi, is the aim of the disciple. This he attempts by the practice of meditation or reverie, or else by the repetition of words. And whilst he is forbidden by the first principles of his faith to do any harm, he is not encouraged to practice any good. We do not wonder, therefore, that the Buddhists are sometimes compared to drones or noxious insects. The character of the Chinese, as a practical and industrious race, forbids them to attach importance to idle and fruitless habits of dreaming away life; but yet, on the other hand, their natural superstition prevents them from wholly discountenancing those who pretend to have magical powers over the elements and the future world,—hence the strange medley of practical common sense and helpless resignation to supernatural influences found among them. The very boatman, who works hard for his few cash, will burn his paper and make the sign with his fingers before he makes his morning venture. And the scholar, who pretends to despise Buddhism and the teaching of Buddha, has got at his fingers' end the sentences contained in the books supposed to possess magical virtue. The present writer had great difficulty in persuading his teacher to go over with him and explain the short *sûtra* known as the "Heart-Sûtra"; but on one occasion, when the book had accidentally been mislaid, he found that the *sin-săng* knew the whole of it by heart, and there was no occasion to seek for the book. And so also, as stated in the early pages[1] of this work, when the Yamên of Yeh Ming-shin, the governor of the two provinces, was entered, in 1857, by the troops under Sir M. Seymour, there was found in the innermost chamber a massive gilt image of Kwan-yin, with the two attendant figures, one on either side; and to all appearances, this image was the object of daily worship to those within the palace. So in practice they contradict themselves.

[1] *Ante*, p. 2.

CHAPTER XXII.

BUDDHISM CONSIDERED PRACTICALLY.

BUDDHISM has sometimes been contrasted with Christianity, as by Mr. Spence Hardy, in his work, called "Christianity and Buddhism Compared." Such a comparison is unnecessary here. The book just named was written for the instruction and guidance of Buddhists; for them the comparison was desirable, but for ourselves, as Christians, it is less so. No one who has studied the question will need to be told that Buddhism is wanting in the great requisites of religion. It fails to meet the case of the world outside "the congregation"; it does not ennoble the daily occupations of busy life by supplying the motive—to please God; nor has it any sufficient power to draw the world back to duty. This power resides in a conviction of God's love. The conviction rests upon a knowledge, founded on reasonable evidence. But Buddhism rests to a great extent on legends,—the ideas of a bygone age. If "the cock to be sacrificed to Æsculapius," like the fly in the ointment, damages the high opinion we might otherwise form of the teaching of Socrates, certainly the legends and fables of Buddhism are equally damaging. They appear to be faded remnants of what was once known or believed to be true. Nevertheless, Buddhism has answered a great purpose in the religious history of the world—nor should we, at any rate as Christians, desire to ostracise it because we are tired of hearing it called Just.

We shall consider, step by step, the influence which Buddhism probably exerted on the prevailing opinions of the Chinese people after its introduction among them.

Confucianism,—which is, in fact, not the teaching of Confucius, but the transmitted doctrine of an early age,—had already shaped itself into a rigid code when Buddha's disciples came to Loyang from India. How would the two systems adjust themselves? The only parts of early Confucianism that require notice are the implied acknowledgment of a belief in a personal God (*Shang-ti*) and the duty of sacrifice. With reference to the belief in Shang-ti, we will follow the steps of a recent writer on the subject in his analysis of this question[1] :—"Attempting to analyse the most important passages of the Chinese classics, with a view to secure correct understanding of the religious ideas of the Chinese, B.C. 2000–1000, on the subject of Shang-ti, we must begin with Yaou and Shun, who lived at the time of Abraham. Shun sacrificed specially to Shang-ti; sacrificed purely to the six honoured ones; offered appropriate sacrifices to the hills and rivers, and extended [his worship] to the host of spirits." This passage (the writer observes) appears to show clearly that Shang-ti is the highest of the invisible powers worshipped by the Chinese 2,000 years B.C. The minister Yu, giving

[1] "China Review," vol. xi., No. 3, p. 162.

advice to the emperor Shun, says: "You will brightly receive gifts from Shang-ti." T'ang, the founder of the Shang dynasty, having summoned his people to attack the tyrant Keē, says: "I fear Shang-ti; I dare not but punish him." When returned to his capital, he says: "The great Shang-ti has conferred, even on the inferior people, a moral sense, compliance with which would show their nature invariably right." Closing his speech, he says: "The ways of Shang-ti are not invariable; on the good doers he sends down all blessings, on the evil doers he sends down all miseries."

After numerous extracts, the writer sums up his argument thus:—"Shang-ti is viewed, in the first instance, as the highest of all spirits to whom the ancient Chinese offered their sacrifices; secondly, as the creator and preserver of all, who has conferred upon men a moral sense; next, as one who governs the world, and can put down mighty kings and exalt them of low degree; next, as one who only wishes to do men good, but punishes the evil doers; next, as one with whom good emperors are after their death; next, as one who by dreams and visions of the night opens the understanding of men; next, as a holy being whom the impure cannot approach; and finally, as one who is also gracious and merciful to penitents. I think every one," he adds, "must say, considering that the ancient Chinese embodied these religious ideas in the term Shang-ti, that we here have the purest idea of God, which a heathen, unaided by special revelation, could possibly attain to."

This writer believes, or is tempted to believe, that

we have, in the Chinese conception of Shang-ti, a literal and exact counterpart of El-eljon, the high[1] God of Melchizedek, a remnant, he thinks, of an older and purer form of worship which may have been preserved through contact with, or tradition derived from, a Semitic tribe dwelling among the Chinese, unless some of the ancestors of the Chinese were themselves descended from Shem.

With reference to this belief, we have seen, in the previous pages, that the Buddhists deny the existence of a personal God.

They attribute creation, as we term it, to the action of fixed laws of destruction and renovation. They say, that it is by the "mutual excitation of wind and water" that everything is changed and renovated, and that the process is an eternal one. They deny, also, that reward comes from God, or punishment; they affirm that actions in themselves bring their results, and that all we do tends to this result. They do not deny the existence of spirits; like the Chinese, they will speak of the six honoured ones, the spirits of hills, and rivers, and trees, and the host of lower spirits occupying the depths beneath; but they will not worship any as the highest of all spirits. The inevitable result, therefore, of contact would be a tendency to lower the conception of Shang-ti; either to fritter it away into "a principle," or to degrade it to a spirit or demon of an order far below the conception of God. And this result, so far as we can gather, did follow: the substitution of a *taou li*, an

[1] Shang-ti means the "high god."

occult principle for an active director and ruler, did take place in the later philosophy, and the worship of spirits in the place of the supreme spirit has become general among the people. Whether this process of decline or degradation would have occurred independently of Buddhist teaching and dogma cannot be determined with certainty. We know that in the time of Confucius such a process had set in, for we are told "he departed from the higher faith of his ancestors, and, by sanctioning the worship of spirits, and omitting all mention of Shang-ti, he reduced that deity to the position of one among the host of heaven. Once only does he speak of Shang-ti . . . . but he deduced nothing from it either to spiritualise his teachings or to elevate his practice."[1] When the denial of God, and therefore of Shang-ti, by the Buddhists, as supreme, added its weight to the growing neglect, it is probable the result to which we have alluded above was at any rate promoted and encouraged.

The old ritual of the Chinese ordained sacrifices. The emperor was commanded to sacrifice to heaven; and at the present day the imperial worship of Shang-ti on the round hillock to the south of the city of Peking is surrounded with all the solemnity of which such an occasion is capable. "The altar is a beautiful marble structure, ascended by twenty-seven steps, and ornamented by circular balustrades on each of its three terraces . . . . Here the emperor kneels, surrounded first by the circles of the terraces and

[1] Douglas, "Confucianism," p. 84.

their enclosing wall, and then by the circle of the horizon.[1] He thus seems to himself and to his court to be the centre of the universe, and, turning to the north,[2] assuming the attitude of a subject, he acknowledges by prayer and by his position that he is inferior to Heaven alone. . . . . As might be expected, careful distinctions are made in the sacrifices. The animals ordinarily used for food by the ancient Chinese, and the fruits of the earth known to them, are almost all included. . . . . But the great distinguishing sign of superiority is the offering of a whole burnt offering to heaven [a first-born male]."

The Buddhists denounce sacrifices. In his interview with the hermits called Bhargavides, on his road to Vaisâlî, the young prince who was to become Buddha, watched their modes of worship and inquired as to their sacrifices. "What is the nature of the religion which consists in offering up sacrifices?" he said. "It is a custom which has been handed down from very remote time," they replied, "that those who worship the Gods must sacrifice." . . . . "I will ask you, then," said the prince, "if a man, in worshipping the gods, sacrifices a sheep and so does well, why should he not kill his child and so do better? Surely there can be no merit in killing a sheep?"

And, consequently, in the Buddhist system all bloody sacrifices are abolished. They offer flowers

[1] Which may have been the ground-work of the old idea of the Holy Chakravarttin, or wheel-king, where the Chakra has been supposed to represent the horizon.

[2] Buddha, also, the great Holy King, like a Chakravarttin, turned his face to the north when he died.

and incense, and sometimes cakes and other food of that sort, but no flesh or the life of any creature.

This, too, would affect the popular belief in China, as it did in India. "The king of Mithila," the Rishis told the prince, "sacrificed to the gods countless victims, hoping to attain the happiness of heaven"; but when Buddhism was established, the great Asoka forbade any creature to be put to death, and went so far, in keeping with his principles, as to establish hospitals, or mercy-houses, for the restoration of sick and wounded animals, and the administration of medicine. So in China, the monasteries are, many of them at least, receptacles for living creatures, who find asylums there. The Haichwang temple of Honan, which has so frequently been described by European visitors, has its special department for "preserving life." And in a popular work, largely circulated among the lower orders, describing the future punishments of the wicked, special wrath is threatened against those "who take life"; whilst the bliss of a happy metempsychosis is freely offered all those who are instrumental in saving the life even of the meanest creature. It is probable that the influence of Buddhism in this particular has been largely felt in China. Although sacrifices are freely offered to Confucius, for instance, of which we read in "The History of the Temples of the Sage,"[1] yet it is impossible to deny that tenderness for life must have been increased among the people by the presence of the vast number of

[1] According to this work, 6 bullocks, 27,000 pigs, 5,800 sheep, 2,800 deer, and 2,700 hares are sacrificed in the temples of Confucius annually. Douglas, p. 165.

Buddhist fraternities in their midst; and, very probably, in the system of sacrifices, which are now very much identified with the burning of paper and the cracking of squibs, at least in the daily and popular worship of the crowds.

But with all the external reverence of the Chinese towards the spirits and demons, and of the emperor towards heaven, there seems to be little of a spiritual or elevating character in their national religion. It is hard and practical. They worship Confucius as devoutly as they adore heaven. "From the time of the Emperor Kaou-Ti (206–194 B.C.) to the present day, Confucius has been, outwardly at least, the object of the most supreme veneration and devout worship of every occupant of the throne. Temples have been erected to his honour in every city in the empire, and his worship, which was originally confined to his native state, has for the last 1,200 years been as universal as the study of the literature which goes by his name. The most important and sacred temple is that adjoining his tomb in Shantung, on which all the art of Chinese architecture has been lavished . . . second only to this temple is the Kwotsze-keen, at Peking, the main difference being that here there are no images. . . . To this temple the emperor goes in state twice a year, and having twice knelt and six times bowed his head to the ground, he invokes the presence of the Sage in these words: 'Great art thou, O perfect sage! thy virtue is full, thy doctrine is complete. Among mortal men, there has not been thine equal. All kings honour thee. Thy statutes and laws have come gloriously down.

Thou art the father of this imperial school. Reverently have the sacrificial vessels been set out. Full of awe we sound our drums and bells.' The spirit being now supposed to be present, the ceremony is gone through of presenting the appropriate offerings, which consist, according to circumstances, of pieces of satin, wine, salted tiger's flesh, dried fish, dried and minced venison, minced hare, minced fish, a pure black bullock, a sheep, or a pig. The officiating mandarin then reads the following prayer: 'On this . . . month of this year, I, the emperor, offer a sacrifice to the philosopher K'ung, the ancient teacher, the perfect sage, and say,—O teacher, in virtue equal to heaven and earth, whose doctrines embrace the past times and the present, thou didst digest and transmit the six classics, and didst hand down lessons for all generations. Now in this second month of spring (or autumn), in reverent observance of the old statutes, with victims, silks, spirits, and fruits, I carefully offer sacrifice to thee! With thee are associated the philosopher Yen, continuator of thee; the philosopher Tsâng, exhibitor of thy fundamental principles; the philosopher Tsze-tsze, transmitter of thee; and the philosopher Mâng, second to thee! Mayst thou enjoy the offerings.'"

This will give an insight into the cold worship and artificial devotion of the national religion of China. The thought is forced on us, as we read the prayer with the context, that a royal toastmaster is apostrophising the spirits of the deceased philosophers, whilst they are being regaled with minced venison, salted tiger's flesh, and wine. And this character seems to pervade the entire system of Confucianism. The Pu-sa, placed in a corner of the room on its tiny altar, with a joss-stick burning before it, is generally a god of wealth or happiness, who is supplicated in a matter-of-fact way for "good custom" and a "lucky bargain"; whilst in the temples the bare tablet, with the inscribed name, is adored as a matter of family business and as a transmitted duty, with no reference to the higher powers of our spiritual nature.

How different this from the worship of the Buddhists! If it be true they worship only a principle, yet it is a principle embodied in a life. The mercy of Kwan-yin was illustrated in the mercy of the living Buddha. Her willingness to save is only the expression of Buddha's aim in being born; not only being born once, but through a succession of ages; and the thought rises even higher, when the recollection of his sufferings for the sake of "all that breathes" is joined with the sentiment of mercy. It is well to recollect the Buddhist theory—for, after all, it is but theory—on this point. The fitness of Buddha to be a supreme teacher consists, not "in his having digested and transmitted the six classics," but in having during a succession of lives perfected himself in the highest morality or moral virtue. He completed the *pâramitâs*, as they are called, and the last of these is the perfection of charity (*dâna*), in completing which he gave up his flesh to feed the hungry tiger-cubs, his eyes to give sight to the blind, his blood to satisfy the ravenous hawk, his head to the king of Taxila, his children, wife, money, and all that he had to the Brahman who begged them. All this may be invention, but it embodies the idea formed of Buddha's character as a teacher—he had done all this and much more, exemplifying his self-sacrificing principles; and when the people bow at his shrine they do, in fact, worship the ideal they have formed of a being clothed with such a character.

We may suppose, therefore, that the introduction of Buddhism among the Chinese tended in some way to elevate their thoughts and give some tinge of spirituality to their worship. At any rate, it must have brought them to a knowledge of a worship distinct from that of the mere powers of nature, or deified intellect, and as it did this, or tends to this, it has answered a great purpose.

The Chinese regard what is called the "superior man" as holding rank next below Confucius. The "sage" was incapable of evil. "Born of a perfectly pure nature, he had but to follow the dictates of his will to walk in the paths of virtue."[1] But the superior man was not so,—he was subject to faults and failings; he was endowed with no special grace by nature, but, by carefully perfecting the good implanted in him, his way became identical with that of heaven, and of earth, and of all things; and he does all this with a view "to give rest to the people."

The Buddhist represents this character in his description of a Bodhisattva. This being has all human qualities, but is possessed of Bodhi, or perfect wisdom. And he exercises this wisdom for the good of others: "having benefited himself, he desires to benefit

[1] Douglas, p. 87.

all,"—this is the phrase usually employed to indicate such a character. The effect of this teaching is exhibited in the fact, that the Chinese, whether Buddhists or not, term their idols or figures by this general term of Pu-sa. It is used for all purposes of this kind, and doubtless the character of the Bodhisattva has been transferred in some degree to these idols. Whether the idea of the "superior man" has been affected by such a definition of the Bodhisattva as we have given is not easy to determine; but the two thoughts, or ideals of human excellence, exhibited by those next in order to the sage run side by side, and, we can hardly doubt, have mutually affected each other.

And as the Buddhist has the "way" for obtaining the character of superiority, or saintliness, so also has the Confucian. It is thus described in the "Book of Great Learning"[1]:—"The ancients, wishing to be sincere in their thoughts, first extended to the utmost their knowledge. Such extension of knowledge lay in the investigation of things; things being investigated, knowledge became complete; this knowledge being complete, their thoughts were sincere; their thoughts being sincere, their hearts were then rectified; their hearts being rectified, their persons were cultivated; their persons being cultivated, their families were regulated; their families being regulated, their states were rightly governed; their states being rightly governed, the whole empire was made tranquil and happy." This tranquillity of the empire was the main

[1] Douglas, p. 92.

object. How different the "way" of the Buddhist:—his aim was to shake off every fetter that kept him in life. The happiness of the world was to escape the joys of any after-life; and the way to this was by the noble path laid down by the Teacher. Here, again, the material aims of the Confucian were brought into collision with the higher and spiritual aspirations of the Buddhist; and, whilst we cannot doubt that there would be an accommodation, perhaps on the one side as well as the other, the direct effect would be to mark out more distinctly the broad line of difference,—hence the angry controversy which sprang up at an early date between the one party and the other, the constant persecution that arose, and the final rejection of the Buddhist creed by the Court.

But, in order to make this more evident, we must explain, in the following section, the ideas of the future immediately following the present life as entertained by the Buddhists in China.

CHAPTER XXIII.

HEAVEN AND HELL.

THERE is a work in the Buddhist collection in China, written by Fa-lin, to confute the sceptical opinions of Fu-yi. Fu-yi was a stern enemy of Buddhism. He lived in the time of the Emperor Kaou-Tsu (A.D. 618–627), the first of the Tang dynasty. He proposed to the emperor that the monks and nuns should be obliged to resume secular life and bring up children, and so benefit the state. "The reason they adopt the ascetic life," he says, "is to avoid contributing to the revenue"; and then he proceeds to accuse the priests of idleness and superstition. To this, it was replied that Buddha was a sage, and it was wrong to speak ill of him; but Fu-yi replied that loyalty and filial piety are the greatest virtues, and that the monks, disregarding both these, were guilty of gross neglect. His opponent, the Buddhist, replied simply by stating that the punishment of hell awaited his vilifier.

The Confucianists do not believe in future punishment—they affect to ignore it; but Buddhist teaching is very distinct on the point. Whence it was derived, is a difficult question to answer, but the effect it has produced, in the case of the lower orders in China, will be seen from what will be said.

The earliest school of Buddhists say, that below the earth there are eight great hells. (1) Sanjiva: the persons born here are provided with iron claws, with which they tear and mangle each other's flesh. Lying on the ground, thus torn and mangled, a freezing wind blows on them. This causes them to revive. The unhappy wretches had thought with themselves "now life is over," but, alas! they have again to endure their torments. Torn and gashed, they are driven from one place to another, till at last they emerge into a frontier place of punishment [a little hell], from which they may be re-born in a higher state. Without describing these places of punishment, we will only add their names as they occur in the books.

(2) The Kâla *sûtra* hell: for disobedience to parents.

(3) The Sanghata hell: for hatred, envy, or passion.

(4) The Raurâva hell: for murderers and poisoners.

(5) Mahâraurava: for heretics and malefactors.

(6) The Tapana hell: for those who have killed animals and roasted or baked them.

(7) Pratapana hell: for apostates.

(8) The Avitchi: here there is no intermission of punishment. It is the lowest of the hells, and allotted for those guilty of reviling Buddha, or shedding the blood of a holy man.

The description given of Avitchi is this:—"It is 8,000 *yojanas* [*yojana* = 6 miles] square, and is surrounded by a sevenfold iron wall. It is full of instruments of torture. When a wicked man is near death, he is hurried off before Jemma, the judge of the dead, who thus addresses him: 'Wicked man! when alive you prepared yourself for hell—disobedient to father and mother, following every kind of false doctrine! Now, then, you shall be condemned to Avitchi.' For innumerable ages [but not interminable] he endures there the dreadful pains of burning and misery. The lictors, seizing their victims, flay them as they stand, and then, holding them down in fiery chariots, convey them thus through the burning streets; ten thousand poisonous blasts assail them on every side; there is no cessation of their pains for a moment, and so it is called the hell with no intermission of pain."

Besides these "great earth-prisons" (the word for "hell," in Chinese, is earth-prison), there are others called frontier or side prisons, through which the sufferers emerge. The time of suffering in each of these places is determined,—after the expiry of the years, the released being may be born either on earth again, as a beast or a man, or else in heaven.

There is no need to describe the heavens of the Buddhists. Those called Kama lokas, which include that of the Olympus-dwelling gods, all admit of the enjoyment of sensuous pleasure. The superior heavens are free from this, and the happiness consists in thought or pure being. The highest heavens admit of no thought, nor do they exclude it; the condition here is purely transcendental.

Such was the belief imported into China when the Buddhist books were brought there. They had known hitherto nothing about such places "in the next world"; Confucius never spake about angels or other spiritual beings; consequently, the Chinese regarded the present life, the happiness of society, as the end of all.

The ground was now changed, and we have seen in the short extract above given, what was the result. Mutual recriminations ensued, and the one party or the other gained the ear of the reigning sovereign and for a time held the upper hand. But the effect of the new religion on the people was to introduce a dread of the hereafter on account of these threatened punishments. There is a book, widely distributed among the people, which relates to this subject,—it is called the "Kin-kong-king-in-kwo-tsiang-chu," or "explanations relating to the causes and fruits [deeds and consequences] of the diamond Sûtra." In this book are pictures of the courts of the infernal regions and the character of the punishments assigned to the culprits brought before the tribunals.

The first illustration, *e.g.*, is of the court "without favour" or partiality. On the judge's seat sits the president of the court; on either side of him is a scroll or inscription—on the left "the earth is a place of yes! yes! no! no!"; on the right "heaven is bright and clear, white and pure." An infernal lictor is dragging a culprit up the stairs, showing his accusation, "he butchered oxen and dogs." On either side stands a grotesque guard, one with a head resembling that of a cow, the other evidently the travesty of a foreigner—supposed to be related to the lower regions. Then we have an account of cases in which this crime of slaughtering animals had brought punishment, and the virtue of saving life had ensured reward.

Throughout the book the eye is pained at the horrible scenes attempted to be drawn—the tortures of the wicked, and the delight of the demons engaged in the disgusting details of dismemberment, disembowelling, and hacking the bodies of their victims. At the conclusion of the work are represented the ten courts presided over by ten judges, of whom the Indian Jemma (Yama), with his two dogs, is the fifth. And, in conclusion, the wheel of metempsychosis is figured, in which we observe no birth as "a *deva*," but only the following: (1) as noblemen; (2) as poor men; (3) born from eggs (birds); (4) apparitional birth (moths, butterflies, &c.); (5) from spawn; (6) from the womb.

These gross exhibitions of the hereafter must tend to lower the tone of the popular mind. It were almost better, we think, that there should be no dread of the future than that it should be so depicted. But the fact remains, that the belief in such punishments awaiting sinful or vicious conduct is generally accepted, and has produced its effects on the ordinary conduct of the people. Whilst it may in some cases prevent crime, it does, nevertheless, produce a debased tone of thought, and foster superstition.

CHAPTER XXIV.

THE TOLERANT SPIRIT OF BUDDHISM.

ONE marked effect on the masses in China resulting from the intermixture of Buddhism with Confucianism and Taouism has been to produce a common indifference to the distinctive character of each. "These three religions," Dr. Edkins says,[1] "are truly national, because the mass of the people believe in them all. They are far from feeling it inconsistent to do so. What is the cause of this indifference? Why do they care so little about finding out what is the truth and holding to it? The reason is this, that the three systems occupy, as it were, the three corners of a triangle,—the moral, metaphysical, and material,—and are supplementary to each other; they are, therefore, able to co-exist without being mutually destructive. It was because Confucianism 'knew God, but did not honour him as God,' that the way was left open for a polytheism like that of the Buddhists." Whether this be so or not, the fact remains, that the majority of people regard with indifference the claims of "contending sects." It seems to the present writer that very much of this is due to the direct to-

[1] "Religious Condition of the Chinese," p. 58.

lerance inculcated by Buddhism, or, at least, preached by the Buddhists. They do not attach weight so much to the doctrine as the life or conduct. If we hang on doctrine, they say, we are depending on a "quality" (*siang*); but the object of religion is to get rid of such dependence, and to free oneself from self-assertion. This spirit of quietism, or indifference, is illustrated by the whole tenour of their history. Passive submission has marked the conduct of the Buddhist wherever he is found, and opposed to this passive condition is all contention for mastery,—hence the mutual accommodation found among the Chinese. Father Huc tells us, in his narrative, how the common reply to all he said about religion was, that the "three doctrines are the same"; and Dr. Edkins gives us a similar assurance. This last writer narrates how he was once expostulating with a poor man who came to the Taouist priest to get a cure for his illness. "At this point the Taouist priest came to the defence of his system. 'You believe in Jesus; we believe in our gods. Religion differs according to place, and every country has its own divinities. Our object is the same as yours,—to make men good. . . . . You honour Jesus, and it is very well for you to do so; but He does not preside over China.'" Such is the mode of thought and style of argument common at the present day with a large class of Chinese priests, and this has been brought about by the co-existence of Buddhism and Confucianism, and the spirit of toleration, or passive indifference, marking the former. This tendency to reconcile the three schools of religion is exemplified in a small work of some popularity in Southern China, written by a scholar, Wu-tsing-tseu, in the first year of Hien-fung. It comprises two treatises, the "Sin-tsung-niu-chi," a Taouist work, and the commentary of Tai-teen, a contemplative priest, on the "Sin-king," the "Heart Sûtra" (pâramitâ hṛidaya Sûtra), a well-known Buddhist book. The aim of this writer is to show that the sayings of Confucius, Laou-tseu, and Buddha all agree in aim and meaning. The one aim is to purify our nature. I have already given a few extracts from this book in another place.[1] But it will be well to bear in mind that this aim or desire to reconcile the three schools is an indication of a growing indifference to all religion strictly so-called, which is, in fact, the characteristic of the Chinese people at the present day.

An important feature in the Buddhist doctrine is the supposed impossibility of the supreme God being capable of causing or allowing suffering. In the Buddhist controversy held at Pantura, in Ceylon, this was the point most frequently urged by the native priests against the Christian doctrine that the Jehovah of the Old Testament was capable of anger and repentance, and that he caused suffering in punishment of sin. Mr. Spence Hardy and other missionaries speak of the dreadful blasphemies of the priests in this particular against the Jehovah of the Old Testament. It is curious that in the controversy of Manes with Archilaus (according to Cyril, vi. 27), the point urged against the God of the Old Testament was, that "He

[1] "Catena of Buddhist Scriptures," p. 280.

was the inventor of evil." It is the characteristic of Buddhism to deplore suffering, and whatever causes suffering, as the one evil,—hence the confusion that has arisen. It is plain, however, that their argument will not bear the test of ordinary experience. Suffering is necessary,—the physician is the cause of suffering, but to do good; yet this commonplace thought does not seem to enter into the mind of the Buddhist; he considers Buddha as the great physician to cure suffering, but in the greater thought of "doing good," the minor necessity, under present circumstances, of bringing good out of apparent evil, has not presented itself.

In China, the universal worship, or honour, paid to Kwan-yin, the Al-makah of Buddhism, is a proof that this idea of mercy is a paramount one in their estimate of divinity. It has been brought about by the "tenderness" of the founder of the system; but it is false; and one great lesson to be welded, as it were, on the mind or conscience of the people who profess Buddhism is, that affliction is sometimes necessary, and chastisement is not a mark of anger or hatred, but of the love of a father who desires to bring out of the suffering peaceable fruits.

The idea of Māra, the evil principle, as first recognised in Buddhism, was that of "death." Māra was lord of the Kama loka, or world of sensual desire, and he is drawn in the Sanchi sculptures as a *deva*, or a being of superior character. There is nothing approaching to the idea of deformity or monstrosity about his appearance; he dwells in the upper world, and not beneath; but this idea was changed afterwards, and in China we have revolting forms of the Prince of Evil presented to us. They were probably derived from later Hinduism. It would be a curious study to trace the connexion between the Assyrian or Babylonian representations of the evil principle through India to China; but, at any rate, there they are, and the popular idea in China of the horrid sprites and diabolical agents that are confederated against our happiness is mainly attributable to corrupt Buddhist teaching; but the earliest idea of Māra was not of this kind—he was the all-powerful ruler of the world, and he exercised his power by promoting the reign of sensual desires.

With respect to its social aspect, the Buddhist doctrine has tended to strengthen ties between parent and child, by representing filial duty as one of the chief virtues. There is a weird sort of story told in the life of Buddha, known as the "Abhinishkramana Sûtra," of a merchant youth who was condemned to wear a red-hot iron ring round his forehead for having struck (or, kicked) his mother; and the duty of obedience and attention to parents is indeed one of the most attractive features in the character of this religion. The youthful Sâma is painted (sculptured) at Sanchi waiting on his blind parents, bringing them fruits and water daily, and because of his piety he was restored to life. So in the history of A*s*oka's son, Kunāla. He had resisted the importunities of his step-mother, and incurred her hatred. He was sent to a distant appenage of the kingdom, and there by her craft his eyes were put out. He submitted to the indignity without complaint, and came playing his lute to the home of his childhood, anxious to know why he had incurred his father's displeasure, but with no resentment. This feature of the Buddhist belief must have recommended the system to the notice of the Chinese, with whom this duty of filial piety is paramount.

And so it would seem that Buddhism not only supplemented the national faith in supplying a metaphysical side to the triangle, but it added in some points to the strength of the morality of the people, and in other points raised and elevated their conceptions. It did nothing, however, to promote the knowledge of the true God, nor has it supplied any substitute for the worship of Shang-ti, the lord and maker of the world; and what it has given in lieu of this, viz., a somewhat meaningless spiritualism, will hardly compensate for the loss of the great thought of a "supreme, personal Ruler" directing and governing the world.

CHAPTER XXV.

BUDDHISM CONSIDERED ÆSTHETICALLY.

THERE is a point of view from which we may regard the result of Buddhism as highly advantageous, that is, in promoting a correct æsthetic taste, especially in religious architecture. Whether it be true or not, that a simple idea underlies all rightly-directed efforts of man to raise a building fit for the worship of God, in this particular Buddhism illustrates the supposed rule, for it was the deep conviction that the highest divinity was not to be figured by any human form or shape that led to the idea of the rounded *topes* and the ascending towers or tees above the *tope*, which called for all the power of man to erect, as the idea had required all his power to conceive.

The Pagoda in China is the expression of the highest expansion of the thought; and nothing, we may say, has more guided and fostered a correct taste in landscape effect and right proportions, combined with beauty of detail, than the almost universal adoption of this Indian model of a Bhagavat, or Pagoda-house.

The symbolism of the *tope* or *stûpa*, from the crowning spire of which the Pagoda originates is, like that of other sacred edifices, intended to figure out an idea of the world, or universe, ruled over or occupied by one supreme spirit or being. This certainly was the meaning of the figure and furniture of the Jewish tabernacle and of the temples. As Josephus says in his "Antiquities, viii., iv., i." : "The odour of the incense in the temple was an indication of God's presence, and of his habitation with men" ; and so, as the same writer observes, Solomon rose up and said, "O Lord! Thou hast an eternal house, and such as Thou hast created for Thyself out of thine own works ; we know it to be the heaven, and the air, and the earth, and the sea," and it was a symbol of this that Solomon built ; so Philo tells us also, and Cosmas labours at length to show the same thing.[1] So likewise the *stûpa* is a high, solid structure, designed to be based on a square foundation or platform, from which rises into the air a semi-circular dome, which is crowned by a square railing, or sometimes a solid cube with eyes on every side. The square platform represents earth, the semi-circular dome figures out air, the railed structure on the top denotes the heaven where watch the four gods (indicated by eyes). This was the first effort to describe in stone the idea of the world, or the three worlds, over which the spiritual presence of Buddha was supposed to rule. In this *stûpa* were his relics, denoting his presence, the only authorised substitute for himself; but, as the system grew, the idea of the universe expanded also, and it was not only earth, and air, and heaven that had to be represented, but the towering worlds above the heaven, and after that the platforms or plateaux (it is

[1] "Topographia," quoted by Yule, Cathay, xlvii.

the only word we can use) of heavens extending upwards and towards the eight points of space,—hence the symbolism expanded also, and above the cubical structure was erected a high staff with rings or umbrellas, to denote world soaring above world to the uppermost empyrean. Now, it is this crowning pole, with its rings or umbrellas, that originated the idea of the Pagoda. Each platform in this structure denotes a world, and, as they tower upwards in beautifully-decreasing size, they offer to the eye an effort of the mind of man to represent in stone the idea of the infinite. On each side of these platforms there are bells and tinkling copper leaves, to denote the eternal "music of the spheres"; and the beautifully-carved balustrades and projecting eaves are ever described as proper emblems of the habitations of the happy beings who enjoy the presence of the Buddhas dwelling in these supernal regions. This is the origin of the Pagodas; and there is nothing which gives China its distinctive architectural character so much as these Buddhist structures, not used for worship, but to figure out the illimitable nature of the space in which dwells the "spiritual essence of all the Buddhas."

From the universal practice of offering flowers at the shrines of Buddha has grown a taste in the cultivation of beautiful flowers and the arrangement of the garden temples which distinguishes the Chinese and the people of Japan. When the present writer was residing at Hakodate, in Japan, he had the opportunity of frequently visiting the temple gardens there and the graveyards in the town. The arrangement of the flowers was a subject of wonder to him,—the varied effects of colour and grouping, and the careful way in which every available corner of ground was utilised for the purpose of cultivation. These flowers were used daily for the decoration of the different altars of the temples; and in the graveyards there were small joints of bamboo sunk in the ground at the head of most of the graves, which were daily filled with water, and a few choice flowers placed therein, by the priests or the deceased one's relatives. In China, this love of flowers, and taste produced thereby in the arrangement of colour and shape, is exhibited in their art and ornamentation on every hand. There is an artificiality sometimes noticeable not found in Japan, but this is just the result we should expect from the unequal division of the public taste between the cramped and artificial ritual of Confucianism and the free and unfettered Buddhism; yet it will not be disputed that the taste is the result of an æsthetic sentiment, excited, in the first instance, by religious conceptions, and sustained and cultured by the growth of such ideas, until it has become natural.

It would be out of our way to describe the effect of Buddhism on the native literature of China; but we may allude to the introduction of the folk-lore of the west among these people. The Jâtakas and other tale-books now form a part of their literature,—these must have had their influence. There is a celebrated tale, translated by Stas. Julien, under the title of "La Blanche et Bleu," of two fairy spirits, or *nâgas*, who carry on a sort of innocent intrigue with a young apothecary of Hankow. This tale is founded on Buddhist story called "Nagānanada," which was probably written at the time of *S*ilâditya Râja, A.D. 650, in India. The ideas run into one another naturally, but the Chinese plot is borrowed from the Indian tale,—and this is true in other points: the tales we find in Æsop are current in China, but in both cases derived from a Buddhist source. Many of these tales appear trivial, but compared with the stories found, for instance, in the "Gesta Romanorum," they are well conceived and sustained, and they must have produced a result, in many cases beneficial, on those who read them.

We sum up, therefore, our estimate of the effect of Buddhism, morally and socially, on the character of the Chinese people in these words:—Whilst it has not answered any great end in raising the religious tone of the masses of the people, it has certainly tended to promote a love of morality, and a healthy state of society, by guarding it against vice or profligacy; and it has helped to raise the mind to a love of the beautiful in nature, and assisted in the advancement of art and literature.

Perhaps, if we were to take the Chinese at the point to which they have advanced—at least, those among them who are Buddhists—and instruct them in a higher wisdom from that point, it would be a right way of using the advantages which their Buddhist culture affords. They are not wedded to idolatry; they have a conception of spiritual truth; they profess to love mercy, and worship an ideal of divine or perfect wisdom. It might be possible to put before them the embodiment of that ideal in the Revelation made to the world of the existence of One who is All-merciful and All-wise.

But here we hold our pen. The remarks already made are designed for the missionary student. If they lead him to consider the subject, or prepare his way for a fuller investigation of it, the purpose of this outline will have been answered.

NOTE A.

THE word Calami, as quoted from Whiston on p. 65, is found to be an error for Calani. Whether Whiston had any authority for his version of the text, I am unable to ascertain. But I think it very probable that "Calami" was the word used by Aristotle. Lassen, in his essay on "Indian Sects noticed by Greek Writers" (in the Rhenish Museum), speaks of the word "Calani" as the invention of some sciolist, derived from the mention of Kalanos in Arrian, and so adapted as the name of a sect. But as we have, in the legend of Gondoforus, the town of Kalamina (see p. 135) named as the scene of the death of St. Thomas, and as this place is generally identified with Potala on the Indus, the seat of the "Sugar-cane" line of kings (the Ikshvâkus), I think it very probable that it was so called from the root Calamus, *the sugar-cane.* In this case the Calami would be the Ikshvâkus.

INDEX.

THE END.

NON-CHRISTIAN RELIGIOUS SYSTEMS.

Fcap. 8vo., Cloth boards, price 2s. 6d. each.

BUDDHISM. Being a Sketch of the Life and Teachings of Gautama, the Buddha. By T. W. RHYS DAVIDS, of the Middle Temple. With Map.

CONFUCIANISM AND TAOUISM. By Professor ROBERT K. DOUGLAS, of the British Museum. With Map.

CORÂN (THE): its Composition and Teaching, and the Testimony it bears to the Holy Scriptures. By Sir WILLIAM MUIR, K.C.S.I., LL.D.

HINDUISM. By MONIER WILLIAMS, M.A., D.C.L., &c. With Map.

ISLAM AND ITS FOUNDER. By J. W. H. STOBART, B.A., Principal, La Martinière College, Lucknow. With Map.

THE HEATHEN WORLD AND ST. PAUL.

Fcap. 8vo., Cloth boards, price 2s. each, with Map.

ST. PAUL IN DAMASCUS AND ARABIA. By the Rev. GEORGE RAWLINSON, M.A., Camden Professor of Ancient History, Oxford.

ST. PAUL IN GREECE. By the Rev. G. S. DAVIES, M.A., Charterhouse, Godalming.

ST. PAUL AT ROME. By the Very Rev. CHARLES MERIVALE, D.D., D.C.L., Dean of Ely.

ST. PAUL IN ASIA MINOR, AND AT THE SYRIAN ANTIOCH. By the Very Rev. E. H. PLUMPTRE, D.D., Prebendary of St. Paul's, Vicar of Bickley, Kent.

RECENT PUBLICATIONS.

---

	s.	d.
BIBLE PLACES; OR, THE TOPOGRAPHY OF THE HOLY LAND: a Succinct Account of all the Places, Rivers, and Mountains of the Land of Israel mentioned in the Bible, so far as they have been identified. Together with their Modern Names and Historical References. By the Rev. Canon TRISTRAM. *Crown 8vo., with Map, numerous Woodcuts ...... Cloth Boards*	4	0
CHINA. By Professor R. K. DOUGLAS, of the British Museum. With Map, and eight full-page Illustrations on toned paper, and several Vignettes. Post 8vo....*Cloth Boards*	5	0
CHRISTIANS UNDER THE CRESCENT IN ASIA. By the Rev. E. L. CUTTS, B.A., Hon. D.D. University of the South U.S., Author of "Turning Points of Church History," &c. With numerous Illustrations. Post 8vo. .... *Cloth Boards*	5	0
INDIA: THE HISTORY OF, from the Earliest Times to the Present Day. By L. J. TROTTER, Author of "Studies in Biography." Post 8vo. With a Map and 23 Engravings .... *Cloth Boards*	10	6
ISRAEL: THE LAND OF. A Journal of Travels in Palestine, undertaken with Special Reference to its Physical Character. Fourth Edition, revised. By the Rev. Canon TRISTRAM. With numerous Illustrations............ *Cloth Boards*	10	6
JERUSALEM: THE SIEGE OF. By the Right Rev. R. S. COPLESTON, Bishop of Colombo. Post 8vo. With an Illustration and Plan of the Temple. .... *Limp Cloth*	1	0
JEWISH NATION: A HISTORY OF THE. From the Earliest Times to the Present Day. By the late E. H. PALMER, Esq., Author of "The Desert of the Exodus." Crown 8vo. With Map and numerous Illustrations......... *Cloth Boards*	5	0
LESSER LIGHTS; or, Some of the Minor Characters of Scripture traced, with a View to Instruction and Example in Daily Life. First and Second Series. By the Rev. F. BOURDILLON, M.A., Author of "Bedside Readings," &c. Post 8vo. ....*Cloth Boards, each Series*	2	6

s. d.

NATURAL HISTORY OF THE BIBLE, THE: being a Review of the Physical Geography, Geology, and Meteorology of the Holy Land, with a description of every Animal and Plant mentioned in Holy Scripture. By the Rev. Canon TRISTRAM. Crown 8vo. With numerous Illustrations. *Cloth Boards* 7 6

NARRATIVE OF A MODERN PILGRIMAGE THROUGH PALESTINE ON HORSEBACK, AND WITH TENTS. By the Rev. A. C. SMITH, M.A., Rector of Yatesbury, Wilts. Crown 8vo. With numerous Illustrations and Four Coloured Plates ......*Cloth Boards* 5 0

PICTORIAL ARCHITECTURE OF THE BRITISH ISLES. With about 150 Illustrations. Letterpress by the Rev. H. H. BISHOP. Royal 4to. ......*Cloth Boards* 4 0

RUSSIA, PAST AND PRESENT. Adapted from the German of Lankenau and Oelnitz. By Mrs. CHESTER. With Map and three full-page Woodcuts and Vignettes. Post 8vo. ......*Cloth Boards* 5 0

SCENES IN THE EAST. Containing Twelve Coloured Photographic Views of Places mentioned in the Bible. By the Rev. Canon TRISTRAM, Author of "The Land of Israel," &c. 4to. ......*Cloth Boards* 7 6

SCRIPTURE MANNERS AND CUSTOMS: being an Account of the Domestic Habits, Arts, &c., of Eastern Nations mentioned in Holy Scripture. Eighteenth Edition. Crown 8vo. With numerous Woodcuts ......*Cloth Boards* 4 0

SINAI AND JERUSALEM; or, Scenes from Bible Lands, consisting of Coloured Photographic Views of Places mentioned in the Bible, including a Panoramic View of Jerusalem. With Descriptive Letterpress by the Rev. F. W. HOLLAND, M.A. 4to. ......*Cloth, Bevelled Boards, gilt edges* 7 6

ST. PAUL: THE CITIES VISITED BY. By the Rev. Professor STANLEY LEATHES, M.A., King's College, London. Fcap. 8vo. With Nine Woodcuts ......*Limp cloth* 1 0

TURNING POINTS OF ENGLISH CHURCH HISTORY. By the Rev. EDWARD L. CUTTS, B.A., Author of "Some Chief Truths of Religion," "St. Cedd's Cross," &c. Crown 8vo. ......*Cloth Boards* 3 6

TURNING POINTS OF GENERAL CHURCH HISTORY. By the Rev. E. L. CUTTS, B.A., Author of "Pastoral Counsels," &c. Crown 8vo. ......*Cloth Boards* 5 0